Teachers, language and learning

Language permeates the curriculum of the school, not only English but Maths, Art, History, Science and so on across the full subject range. This book looks closely at what this means by focusing on the activities over a six year period of a secondary school's Language and Learning Committee. It shows what happens when teachers come together to formulate their own research agenda, engage in the observation of each other's classrooms, read together, and reflect upon their theory and practices by taking part in informal seminars. It describes both the success and setbacks of such an enterprise, and will be of great interest to teachers at all levels as well as to student teachers.

The chapters by the book's editors offer a linking narrative for the teachers' voices and refer outwards to the broader context of whole-school issues: linguistic diversity, relations with the local community, race and gender. Chapters by the teachers explore the vital relationship between language and learning in subject teaching and examine ways of supporting second language learners and those with special learning difficulties.

Taken as a whole the book provides a model of collaborative, professional development which is a powerful challenge to any who claim that standards can be raised simply by increasing central control over the curriculum and by imposing external attainment targets on students and teachers.

The Editors

John Hickman is Head of English at Forest Gate Community School in East London, where he is also Senior Teacher responsible for in-service training, student teachers and new teachers.

Keith Kimberley is Lecturer in the Department of English and Media Studies, and in the Centre for Multicultural Education, University of London Institute of Education. From 1964 to 1979 he taught English in ILEA secondary schools.

Contributors

John Hickman, Tony Jones, Keith Kimberley, Dave Lewis, Jon McGill, Elaine Mount, Wendy Parmley, Nicki Regan, Pat Roberts, Harold Rosen, Chrissy Smith, Erika Shaw

Routledge Education Books

Advisory editor: John Eggleston
                   Professor of Education
                   University of Warwick

Teachers, language and learning

Edited by
John Hickman
Keith Kimberley

Routledge
London

First published in 1988 by
Routledge
11 New Fetter Lane, London EC4P 4EE

© *1988 John Hickman and Keith Kimberley*

Typeset by Columns of Reading
Printed and bound by
The Guernsey Press Co. Ltd., Guernsey, Channel Islands.

British Library Cataloguing in Publication Data

Teachers, language and learning.—
  (Routledge education books).
  1. Education. Role of Language
  I. Hickman, John II. Kimberley, Keith
  370

ISBN 0-415-03150-8 (c)
     0-415-00870-0 (p)

We dedicate the book to all students of Forest Gate Community School past, present, and future for whom this work was undertaken.

Contents

Contents

Acknowledgments

As well as the people who have written chapters for this book, there are many people who have made contributions to the work described. Most important are those who have worked on the committee during its six years of existence:

Bernice Adkins, Home Economics; Taskeen Bakht, Science; Ian Binnie, History; Barbara Burke, Special Needs; Mukhtar Chahal, Science; Brian Clark, Science; Phil Crawford, CDT; Lynda Donaldson, English; Greta Edwards, Modern Languages; Maggie Farrar, ESD/ ESL; Bill Ferrier, History; Mike Foley, Sociology; Alan Fuller, ESD; Shirley Gibson, History; John Harris, Careers; Paul Harwood, Maths – Deputy Head; Moira Hawley, Modern Languages/ESL; Ted Henderson, RE; Barbara Holden, Community Outreach Teacher; Linnet Jones, English/Pastoral; Rosemary Lucas, ESL; Jo Lumsden, English; Rosemary Lyons, English/RE; Yvonne Marson, PE; Keith Mears, Geography; John Mills, English; Hazel Newman, Maths; Srima Perera, Science; Naz Rassool, ESD; Pete Reay, CDT; Sandie Reid, Maths; Robin Rice, RE; Dave Thomas, Science; Jill Wallis, ESD; Jacky Westgarth, HE; Jane Wray, PE.

We would also like to thank Jean Bleach, and the Schools' Council Project Language for Learning, Mark Cremin and Newham Talk and Learning Project, The London Association for the Teaching of English, John Widdowson for his help with the history of Newham, Mrs Anne Rowland for her advice and support, and Christina Pulle and Pat Bennet for their help with the manuscript.

Contributors

John Hickman is Head of English at Forest Gate Community School and is Senior Teacher with responsibility for staff development and for students and probationary teachers.

Tony Jones is Head of Maths at Forest Gate Community School.

Keith Kimberley is Lecturer in the Department of English and Media Studies at the London University Institute of Education including a part-time responsibility in the Centre for Multicultural Education.

Dave Lewis is a lecturer in Further Education. He was previously Head of English at McCentee School in the London Borough of Waltham Forest and, prior to that, Second in the English Department at Forest Gate Community School.

Jon McGill is Head of Third Year at Chase Cross School in the London Borough of Havering. He was previously Head of Year at Forest Gate Community School and taught in the History Department.

Elaine Mount is responsible for primary-secondary liaison at McCentee School in the London Borough of Waltham Forest and was previously the Head of Educational Support and Development Department at Forest Gate Community School.

Wendy Parmley is Coordinator of the Euston Sixth Form Consortium in the Inner London Education Authority. Previously she taught French and English as a Second Language at Forest Gate Community School and was Assistant Head of Sixth Form.

Nicki Regan is a teacher of English at Forest Gate Community School.

Pat Roberts is Headteacher of Langdon Park School in the Inner London Education Authority and was previously Deputy Head at Forest Gate Community School.

Harold Rosen is Emeritus Professor of Education at London University Institute of Education.

Erika Shaw is a teacher of Art at Forest Gate Community School.

Chrissy Smith is a teacher of English and Drama at Forest Gate Community School and was previously a primary teacher at Upton Cross Junior School.

Preface

This book began when a small group of teachers working in a school to the East of London agreed to write down talks they had given to a cross-curricular committee. It grew because other teachers followed their example and because some teachers in the school undertook small-scale investigations of their classroom practice. Slowly, almost imperceptibly at times, the book has become a record of activities across a period of six to seven years, charting ideas and initiatives in the general territory of language and learning. It now ranges widely into many aspects of the school's curriculum and organization but retains at its centre a concern to understand how students learn and how teachers can best support them.

We think that this produces, as a result, a book which, in telling a particular story, produces insights which have considerable generalizability and is likely to be of interest to teachers at several levels. It should for instance, be of interest to headteachers and senior staff responsible for curriculum development as it suggests ways in which teachers can be encouraged to evaluate the learning that goes on in their classes and to take part in the processes by which change comes about in a school. It should be of interest to teachers in general who will, we trust, see themselves and their concerns represented in the teachers' accounts of their practice. It should also be of interest to students on BEd and PGCE courses both as a way into understanding the schools where they go for practical teaching experience or will begin teaching in as probationers, and as a means of appreciating the diverse strands of activity which go to make up a school's language policy.

Despite much talk about language policies since the publication of *A Language for Life* (The Bullock Report) (DES, 1975), there are very few examples of the long-term development of language policies and still fewer documented accounts of the processes involved.

We have attempted to unfold this longer-term history, including the false starts and failures. The reader needs to know that we are not interested in Utopian schemes and unrealizable ends but have attempted to record what teachers can do in everyday circumstances, often against the odds.

When Professor Rosen agreed to write the initial chapter, he pointed out to us the importance of our 'double focus': on the learning of both students and their teachers. We hope that readers will find a proper balance between these concerns. Our intention has been, on the one hand, to catch the teachers' voices; to capture the imagination and commitment that, given the opportunity, they devote to teaching; and to describe the role they can play in shaping policy. The book demonstrates, we think, the importance of giving teachers responsibility and respecting their abilities and 'goodwill'. On the other hand, however preoccupied we may appear to be at times with the dilemmas teachers currently face, it is the students' learning (and barriers to it) which is at the centre of this book and gives it its *raison d'être*. The activities of the Language and Learning Committee described in these pages take their energy from a common desire among those involved to understand the texture of what goes on in their classrooms. They were kept going in their writing by an interest in the students they teach and a fascination with what they discovered when they got close to the experiences of the children and young people in their care. The detail in later chapters is more than support for general arguments; it is the driving force which powers those arguments forward.

The contributors to this book mainly have focused on aspects of language and learning but, as you will see from the interlinking chapters, broader social issues have played a significant role in the school's intellectual life, influencing policy and practice. Discussions of race and gender, in particular, have played an important part in generating new approaches to parents and the community and in bringing about changes in the curriculum. For our part, we have divided and shaped the material into sections which we hope will give the book coherence but we would be the first to acknowledge that we have imposed order which is uncharacteristic of the ways in which change takes place in schools. We are also aware that we may have fixed into a single mould the history of the Language and Learning Committee and recognize that, however hard we have tried to let the voices of those involved speak for themselves, we know that we, as editors, act as a filter through which their accounts are perceived. Just as the Committee was to decide that 'going public', even to the whole staff, is not always desirable, so we need to remind the reader and ourselves that processes which seem to work best when informal and unpressured, cannot adequately be captured in a history compiled long after the events it describes.

We think this is a positive book but, we hasten to add, it does not ignore the dilemmas which face any school which is attempting to develop its curriculum, undertake research, and engage in in-service programmes at a time of expenditure cuts, falling rolls, and the imposition of both a national curriculum and a contract defining teachers' conditions of service by a government broadly hostile to teachers. Forest Gate Community School is typical of secondary schools all over the country and we think the value to the reader will lie in the description of recognizable processes and realizable practices. We hope we have achieved a fair amount of realism. We would not wish to pretend that all teachers agree about how children learn or about what should be given emphasis in their teaching. Nor do all teachers want to work collaboratively.

There are few books in the literature of education which try to record the processes which operate simultaneously at classroom and school level over a long period of time, so there are no established ways of reading this book. We hope that readers will not treat it as a curriculum project to be evaluated, nor a model, or series of models, to be copied. We would prefer people to sift our account for what is useful to them, using it as a means of reflecting on, and seeking to change, their own circumstances. There are no obvious 'therefores' from this history. Teachers and schools must make their own decisions in relation to their own specific histories and contexts. Rarely in the history of public education can it have been more important than it is now for teachers to insist upon their professional competence; make links with parents and the community; and demonstrate that standards are raised, not by external attainment targets, but by having a teaching profession which cares about, and has high expectations for, the students they teach.

John Hickman
Keith Kimberley
October 1987

Note: In writing the linking chapters, we have used a personal style, using 'we' both to refer to ourselves and the Language and Learning Committee. We hope that this will not be confusing and will serve to acknowledge that, in writing about activities with which we have been connected closely for a long period of time, we cannot claim the objectivity which the use of impersonal forms might imply.

Chapter 1

Language across the curriculum: a changing agenda

Harold Rosen

Standing behind this book is an important piece of educational history. Some of it has never been written – at least in any public form. For me this history is personal since I was very close to many of the events which were central to it. How does it belong with this book? The protracted endeavours described here, warts and all, are not only a record of a unique achievement in one school, but also grew out of a decade of attempts to put life and meaning into what has now become one of those much bandied about phrases or slogans which resound through the educational world – language across the curriculum (wisely translated by the teachers at Forest Gate School to 'language and learning'). There had been conferences, courses, books, official pronouncements and local authority promotion before the teachers who write here got down to the difficult business of realizing in one place the translation of general policies into classroom practices. There were also, as always happens, particular individuals who were the carriers of ideas from 'outside' to the discussions reported in these pages.

One more preliminary. Amongst all the publications which flood the educational market it is all too rare to find close-focus accounts of attempts to innovate in one school. It is even rarer to find accounts written by the participants themselves. This is true of language across the curriculum. It becomes clearer every day that the enthusiasm and years of sustained work which went into attempts to turn language across the curriculum from a piety into working practices is being largely ignored in the government's proposals for a national curriculum, in the terms of reference of the Kingman Committee and in proposals for national testing. All this gives this book a special importance. We will need to turn to it (and others) because the philosophy it represents will not lie down and die. Teachers will see to that. And we can take heart from the fact that alongside current central government policy we have had the National Writing Project and the beginning of the National Oracy Project. The latter offers as two of its three aims:

- to enhance the role of speech in the learning process, 3 to 19, encouraging active learning across the curriculum
- to develop the teaching of oral communication skills across the curriculum

(SCDC 1987)

Thus in its very first document it declares that it will place 'particular emphasis on process materials geared to school-based teacher development'.

I think I know where the central ideas of language across the curriculum were born. Back in the 1960s the London Association for the Teaching of English (LATE) found itself breaking out of the boundaries which had usually defined the concerns of teachers of English. We stopped minding our own business and ventured into discussing language in education, language and experience, language and thought. For we had begun to realize that some goals could never be reached if we continued to regard language as something which happened only in five or so lessons each week. We turned our attention to the integrated curriculum, group work, environmental studies; beginning to scrutinize more closely the ways in which pupils encountered and used language throughout the school day.

Much of this will sound familiar and possibly commonplace today but twenty years ago these themes were radically new and there was very little to turn to other than our small-scale investigations and explorations, a hint here and there and some powerful theory about language and learning in scholars like Vygotsky (scarcely known at that time), Piaget and Bruner. These theoretical insights would not have flavoured our sessions if it had not been for the work of James Britton, his colleagues and teachers/students at the Institute of Education. At that time his work was known to us by word of mouth for he had not yet published *Language and Learning* (Britton, 1970). Perhaps this would all have had very little impact and the excited arguments of a few dozen teachers would have evaporated. But we began on this in 1966 when the reappraisal of the curriculum and ways of learning began to climb to the top of the educational agenda and, though we were largely unaware of it at the time, a new receptive audience was coming into being.

2

This was the period when the tape recorder was coming into its own. Our discussions were based on tapes which we had made of children talking in different situations and some of our assumptions were rudely challenged by what we heard. In those days it was possible to write books about children's language and indeed about language in general without including a single transcript of real live talkers. We began with talk, seeing it as at the heart of learning and discovering ways in which it was managed in the classroom. The culmination of two years' activity came in May 1968. We wanted to make an impact, to achieve a wider dissemination of our ideas. We set about formulating a manifesto which would be relevant to teachers of subjects other than English. It was produced in the heat of our discussions by five groups in half a morning, typed and duplicated in a lunch hour, finally stitched together and edited by a small committee. It was a prodigious effort by forty or so teachers. To the best of my recollection it was at that weekend conference that the phrase 'language across the curriculum' was born.

How did we propose to disseminate our ideas? We were fortunate in having eagerly ready Martin Lightfoot of Penguin Books. In 1969 he published *Language, the Learner and the School* (Barnes et al., 1969) which contained a research report by Douglas Barnes on 'Twelve Lessons in the First Term of Secondary Education', a piece by James Britton called 'Talking to Learn' and a short piece which I wrote on behalf of LATE to introduce 'A Language Policy Across the Curriculum'. The success of the book in terms of its circulation, national and international, took us by surprise given the modest circumstances in which it had been born. In 1971 a new and revised version was published and I expanded the few pages introducing the language policy document to some fifty which I more cautiously entitled *Towards a Language Policy Across the Curriculum*. It included some discussion of theory and of the ideas generated by the first edition and a much revised version of the policy proposals which now concluded,

> Arising from discussion and investigation it should be possible for some schools to put into operation a language policy which would act as a guide to all their teachers. Such a policy would, of course, be developed and modified in the light of the experience gathered from its formulation and application and would, therefore, be shaped to meet the needs of specific schools.

We know now, for we have learnt the hard way, that to embark on both the formulation and application of a language policy in a school is to tread a long hard road. This book from Forest Gate School takes us down that road. But we knew back there in 1971 that it would be fatal to propose a policy suited to every school, a Platonic blueprint.

Here too this book shows how true this is. A warning to those assiduous compilers of guidelines, objectives and national curricula.

The Bullock Report (*A Language for Life*, DES, 1975) gave its blessing to language across the curriculum. In Chapter 12 (pp. 118-193) we find,

> We strongly recommend that whatever the means chosen to implement it a policy for language across the curriculum should be adopted by every secondary school.

Such a recommendation could easily be a mixed blessing. Indeed some authorities, in their eagerness to toe the line, made peremptory demands that schools hand over a language policy in short order! At Forest Gate, we can see a delicate awareness of some of the less desirable consequences of the Bullock Report's blessing. Indeed they went further and, from the outset, declared their intention 'to explore processes rather than write a policy'. (p. 24). This may well be one of the most important pointers of the book. The documents which constitute this book create a different universe from one which issues marching orders. Though our original intention of dramatizing the issues through the language policy document may have been right at the time, we should now give them a different emphasis, much more like Forest Gate's – share, discuss, investigate, report, propose. But remember that the Bullock Report gave a mere five pages of its 600 to language across the curriculum. Yet the impact of that short chapter was enormous. It stimulated discussion at all levels and set in train many initiatives in many schools.

Yet when all is said and done the results overall were disappointing. In *Bullock Revisited* (Department of Education and Science, 1982) a certain disenchantment was very evident. The Forest Gate teachers could tell you why. They would be the last to set themselves up as a model. But what they demonstrate by their evidence and their appraisal of it is that, even with their refined and principled tact, the process of working on language and learning within one school is slow and to some extent unpredictable. Success turns on the style of work which teachers settle for, not one which an authority, however benign, dictates to them. They show further that their growth of understanding was much more than hoisting themselves up by their bootstraps. They were in touch. By 1980, it was possible to link up with other activities of various kinds. They may well insist that their school is ordinary. I think that they are right. But we have to seek for those forces at work which enabled them to carry on from 1980 to 1987 and, indeed, to emerge with a serious and important publication at the end of it.

The work undertaken did not consist of individualistic fantasies nor did it exist simply within one school. It took place in relation to a back-drop of local and regional involvements, national research projects, subject associations, and, for many individual teachers, wove into their studies for award-bearing courses. The precise details of this back-drop emerge in the text again and again. There were teachers in the school who had connections with a network in which language across the curriculum was quietly being revised, expanded and rewritten. Why was that necessary?

I leave aside the fact that, in 1969, and even in the Bullock Report, the ideas were largely programmatic. To be more precise there was no living example which could be cited of a school which by one means or another had made language and learning a significant feature of its planning. In the intervening decade, new and burning issues forced themselves onto the agenda. When we set out our proposals, we were fully conscious of the fact that most schools had no agenda in the sense of a more or less democratic machinery created for the discussion and planning of the curriculum. All that changed. In this sense Forest Gate was, as the teachers insist, 'ordinary'. Documented meticulously here is the process by which the teachers fashioned an apparatus suited to the complex ideas which they wanted to pursue, shaped to enable them to teach each other and to help them 'become their own experts'. This documentation is the more important because it records frankly the stumblings, the reservations, the disagreements. We would learn less from it if it did not. The staff booklet on talking and learning never got beyond the introduction! The record of attempts to get down to some theoretical reading (ambitious, even avant-garde) reveals how an apparently splendid idea can partly founder when it meets reality.

But let me return to the new agenda of the 1970s. We know it now almost as an incantation: racism, gender, and class. These were the thundering silences in our efforts of the 1960s, which were guilty of assuming a basically benign context for innovation. It was as though we assumed that if only people could be persuaded that talk in the classroom was a liberating force, that writing for real purposes would help students to learn, that the reader was an active creator of meaning, that students could help each other to learn – then all would be well. Needless to say those ideas and others still need promoting, enriching, and modifying. They remain firmly at the heart of the enterprise and at Forest Gate we can see that process at work. But we can also see the new agenda surfacing.

As the teachers settled down to their discussions, they did so well aware that another slogan-programme was filling the air. It was called multicultural education and, like language across the curriculum, was being promoted at all levels and in various forms. Even the DES, in muted and cautious language, gave it currency. But the teachers would also have been conscious of the scepticism and hostility, particularly in the black community, which insisted that the core issue was racism and how to combat it in schools. Jon McGill's paper (cited in Chapter 4) shows how early in its life the Language and Learning Committee addressed the question. Racism is not matter of language alone; yet language is installed in it whether we are looking at minority languages, the prejudices and vicious myths incorporated in the English language, or how all kinds of school texts transmit and perpetuate a white racist view of the world. The images, icons, assumptions, and references of racism stalk the pages of texts we turn every day. Jon McGill urged his colleagues to address matters of this kind:

> . . . it is pointless to abdicate the responsibility of suggesting how we might better inform ourselves, how we might be more aware of the interference of our own prejudices or standards in the education of all children. . . (p. 37).

It is clear from Jon McGill's paper and many other passages in the book that the language issues linked to racism belong with an awareness of linguistic diversity. Schools were slow to come to terms with the dramatically new configurations in the language repertoire of their students. The presence of speakers of dozens of languages and dialects had of course been registered but remained unstudied and unreflected on. The drive was to teach them English as fast as possible and, in the 1970s, the ESL teacher became a familiar figure in the schools.

Slowly a change became perceptible not unconnected with the growing awareness of racism. It manifested itself as an effort to uncover the 'basic facts', to discover which languages and dialects were spoken by the school population, by how many of them, to what extent, and for what purposes. The answer to these simple questions turned out to be very complicated as we discovered when we set about the survey reported in *The Languages and Dialects of London Schoolchildren* (Rosen and Burgess, 1980), to be followed by the much larger-scale investigation by the Linguistic Minorities Project reported in *The Other Languages of England* (Linguistic Minorities Project, 1985). But these investigations were much more than surveys. We set out in a final chapter the educational implications of our findings and the researchers of the Linguistic Minorities Project, through their dissemination wing (LINC), did the same. Both these projects were known to the teachers at Forest Gate through the fine web which connected them with the world of research via individuals and organizations.

The presence of large number of students of Asian and Caribbean origin would have made it almost inevitable that the teachers would address the linguistic diversity under their noses. What was by no means so inevitable was that they would do so with such high awareness. I see none of the glib assent to comfortable formulae in their deliberations. Naz Rassool epitomizes this with her insistence that the rationale of bilingualism cannot be a comfortable pluralism but that language learning must 'challenge the predominantly monocultural and monolinguistic perspectives' (cited in Chapter 15, (p. 137). Forest Gate teachers were thus both inhibiting and contributing to a linguistic awareness which made the early 1970s look distant and insensitive. So we find in this book an account of a vigorous Bilingualism Working Party; and a readiness to take on a new approach to English as a Second Language, shifting it to the mainstream classroom. There is a glimpse of a first-year English programme which includes the Forest Gate Language Survey (see Document 4 in the Appendix) and of 'Community' language provision in the fourth- and fifth-year curriculum.

Of course linguistic diversity is not only about readily perceived languages and dialects. Diversity is in each one of us and in apparently homogeneous communities. Nowhere is this more apparent than in social class variation and the role of Standard English. Throughout the 1970s, the educational significance of the relationship between language and class was the battleground for a major clash. What was it all about? Fundamentally it was about the educability of working-class children, contrasted unfavourably with middle-class children. It was a battle between those who regarded working-class language (whatever that was – dialect? code?) as an inadequate instrument for learning and those who not only saw it as adequate but possessing its own strengths.

I oversimplify in those brief sentences and refer to the issue for one reason alone. I find very little direct attention given to it by the Forest Gate teachers. I get a sense that they had left all that behind them, had taken a stance before the Language and Learning Committee came together. Or it may be that the 'old' issue of language and class was now subsumed under wider concerns. Indeed, my feeling is that the teachers just assume their students are as capable of learning as any others. They concentrate on how best to foster that learning. If I am right, then what the teachers seem to be saying, but only implicitly, is, 'We finished that item of the agenda before we began on ours.' The issue will not, of course, go away as a matter of *general* concern. It haunts the pages of *English 5 to 16* (Department of Education and Science, 1984) just as it did the Bullock Report. Linguistic deprivation, as it came to be known, seems to be a non-issue at Forest Gate at least in the activities of the Language and

Learning Committee; what the non-participants thought is another matter.

It is a tribute to the growth of feminism in the country at large, and amongst teachers in particular, that after 1970 it became almost impossible to engage in serious educational discussion without including gender. To go back before that date is to discover that gender questions had left the schools virtually untouched. A re-reading of my own, and like-minded colleagues', pre-1970 publications is embarrassing. Yet it comes as no surprise that one of the sub-groups concerned itself with issues of gender and race. They had at their disposal a host of reports and studies which showed beyond doubt that in the management of classroom discourse (who is listened to, what is ignored), in the selection of texts, in the texts themselves, in subtle ways of transmitting expectations, sexism was the order of the day in schools.

The ways in which the wider discourse of the educational world found its way into the Language and Learning Committee can be found in every chapter. Against their preoccupations, the priorities being put before us at this moment seem like irrelevancies but for the power which sustains them. The teachers do not spend their time debating which grammar items should figure in the curriculum nor how they might best conduct tests of language development at 11, 14, and 16. On the contrary, they look to the outside for work which gives them deeper understanding.

Let me take just one example. We know a lot more now about language in classrooms. It is true that some linguists and sociologists pursue their researches in classrooms in order to address their own disciplines and with no concern for questions of learning. On the other hand we can point to Douglas Barnes' development from the work reported in *Language, the Learner and the School* (Barnes et al., 1969) to that reported in *Communication and Learning in Small Groups* (Barnes and Todd, 1977). The titles tell all. Edwards and Furlong (1978) have argued fully on the basis of their classroom evidence in the *Language of Teaching* that:

> . . . teachers can never actually *transmit* knowledge, for they are still dependent on the pupil undertaking his own interpretive work and making the necessary links for himself. Only by engaging in this essentially creative process can he enter the teacher's system of meanings. Only in this way can he learn.

There are echoes there of the stance taken on language and learning right from the beginning. The difference lies in the fact that Edwards and Furlong base their conclusion on the fine detail of their classroom evidence. The work continues, as we can see from the socio-psychological approach of Edwards (a different one) and Mercer in

Common Knowledge: The development of understanding in the classroom (Edwards and Mercer, 1987). I drop these few names (many more could be cited) to indicate that we have come a long way and stand on stronger ground. The intellectual and theoretical base for work like that of the Language and Learning Committee is wide and deep and teachers should know it. I might, with more space, have shown how the same is true of our understanding of the reading process and the role of the reader, the act of writing, and advances in the understanding of the relationship between language and thought.

In spite of attempts to exile it from official pronouncements, the concern for language and learning will not go away. This account of how teachers undertake for themselves the same kinds of learning processes as those they hope to develop with their students will help us to ensure that that will be so. For we have presented here a unique compilation which gradually lays bare the intricacies of trying to convert high aspirations into working practices. It is a unique record but not a unique experience. We need particularly strongly at this time to tell each other the stories of our lives in teaching and to remind those who propose from afar what life in schools is really like. Had we known at that weekend conference that what we were saying would make a contribution to the coming into being of this book we would have been incredulous but thrilled. And there's a moral in that.

Chapter 2

Community, school, and language

John Hickman and Keith Kimberley

By recording and discussing work done at a particular state secondary school, Forest Gate School in the London Borough of Newham, we are aware, as authors of the linking chapters, that we could easily fall into the trap of writing a narrowly-focused account of little interest to anyone but the participants in the processes we are describing. It is our intention to avoid this and we hope that arguments will be widely applicable.

This said, we wish to acknowledge that our account takes its strength from its particularity. The processes and issues discussed in this book have been generated by people working together in one place, in a particular historical context both local and national, and in a specific set of social and economic circumstances. We hope that we have been able to show how general issues can be given a 'local habitation and a name' and how, conversely, the examination of concrete examples raises issues which can inform analysts and planning.

This chapter suggests how local and national issues interweave in the shaping of a school's activities. It also discusses the relationship between school and community and the difficulty of defining what 'community' means when applied in the area of Newham from which Forest Gate School draws its students.

Community

There is no single meaning which can be attached to the word 'community'. It can, for example, be used as a broad term to refer to all the people who live in a district or locality. This is a territorially-based description in which 'local community' perspectives are distinguished from national ones and schools are seen as part of, and expected to respond to, formal patterns of local government organization. This meaning would here refer to all the people who live, work, pay rates, and vote in local elections in the London Borough of Newham.

Another set of meanings of community refers less to locality and formal relationships and more to shared concerns. This sense of the word can be used to describe the relationships based on interests which people see themselves, and are seen by others, as having in common. In any 'local community' there may thus be groups of people whose lives are linked together in close relationships for various reasons, (class, cultural or religious background, among others). Such groups have a strong sense of common concerns which are not necessarily shared with, and may be antagonistic to, other groups. The values of an entrenched group can also be in opposition to the publicly known values of the local community at large on certain issues. We will need to consider further the importance of the distinctive identities of such groups within any discussion of the community as a whole.

In our use of the word, we have found it important to draw on both of these areas of meaning. For a start the majority of the parents who make up part of the 'local community' in Newham send their children to locally administered state primary and secondary schools. These schools are theirs both with respect to their children's education and through the policies of local government. What happens in a school like Forest Gate, as we discuss later in this chapter, is substantially influenced by the policies of the London Borough of Newham.

However, we also think it is useful to focus on the second sense of the word especially since, despite the mythologies concerning the cohesiveness of East London communities, we are convinced that neither Newham, nor the somewhat smaller area of the Borough from which the School largely draws its students, can be regarded as a single community, in the sense of a network of relationships marked out from other communities by shared values and concerns.

In economic terms, as Rosalind Yarde points out in an article in *The THES* (3.7.87) on Newhams' Community College and Schools:

> The borough is a patchwork quilt of the poor, the comfortably off, and the soon-to-be-rich.

She quotes Ruth Silver, deputy Principal of the Community College, who comments on the problems involved in identifying a unified set of community interest:

> to talk of community in a borough so socially, economically and structurally divided as Newham is little more than 'pie in the sky' . . . with the advance of 'yuppiedom' and the retreat of close-knit streets and minds, the idea of community if it ever existed, is in danger of becoming extinct.

11

We ourselves do not, of course, wish to deny that the vast majority of the people of Newham have common interests and concerns but it is important to note that the community is made up from diverse strands, containing certain distinct groups as well as people who are not strongly connected with local networks of relationships. Schools like Forest Gate Community School need to identify the many strands which make up the local community, or communities, in which they are set. They have to decide how to respond to conflicts of interest between groups as well as building on shared concerns. We note, with Ruth Silver, the changes now taking place and that the differences and contradictions of the inner cities are likely to increase rather than decrease in the future, increasing the contrast between the wealthy and the deprived, between the secure and the victimized.

Employment, health and housing

Newham took its present name from the amalgamation of East and West Ham in 1965. Although its growth in the eighteenth century depended upon its importance as a market gardening area, its industrial roots go back to 1839 and the opening of the railway through Stratford. This was followed by the establishment of the Royal Docks in 1855, of the Tate and Lyle sugar refineries in the 1880s, and of Beckton Gas Works, which became one of the largest employers of labour in south-west Essex. This long industrial heritage has been eroded over the last twenty years by the closure of the Royal Docks and a general exodus of large-scale industry. This is now reflected in an unemployment rate of more than 22 per cent and a quality of housing and health care which falls below that of most other areas in the country. The population, which reached a peak of 440,000 in 1925, has fallen ever since and now, according to the 1981 Census, stands at about 210,000. Between 1971 and 1978 30 per cent of all manufacturing jobs were lost to the borough and in 1981, 59 per cent of workers living in North Forest Gate worked outside Newham.

In the central Newham area more than half the jobs fall into three categories: shopping and distributive trades; manufacturing; and car repairs and miscellaneous services, but in the Stratford employment area, which includes Forest Gate, the unemployment rate at the time of writing is now nearly 21 per cent, with male unemployment running at 25 per cent. In October 1982, there were 80 unemployed people for every vacancy and, although the 16-24 age range represents 25 per cent of the workforce, it makes up 40 per cent of the unemployment total.

It is also worth mentioning that in terms of health and housing Newham appears to suffer in comparison to other parts of the country. The mortality rate is 15 per cent higher than for the country as a whole; whilst the number of deaths at birth or in the first week after birth is 55 per cent higher than for the country as a whole. About 9 per cent of households in central Newham have no bath, 12 per cent have no inside w.c. and just over 10 per cent are designated as overcrowded.

From this kind of statistical information, an outsider might, rightly, take away a picture of depressingly low student morale, but, although there is a powerful awareness of the shadows cast by unemployment and a depressed economy, the expectations of a large proportion of the school population seem to be surprisingly high. School students' faith in what a 'good' education can achieve for them has, perhaps a little naively, been preserved despite the upheavals of recession:

> What I expect my school to do for me is to help me get all the qualifications I need for the job that I want when I grow up.
> (Fourth-year-girl)

> I would like to achieve a great deal from school: for example 'O' levels and 'A' levels, but whether I can actually do it is another matter. School, to me, is very important, as it moulds your future. If you don't do well at school the chances are you won't do well in later life.
> (Fourth-year boy)

> What I hope from my school is some 'O' levels so that I can walk out of it and get a job straight away. I know its highly unlikely but I hope it will happen.
> (Fourth-year boy)

Whether the advent of an airport for short take-off aircraft, luxury hotels, and new rail links to the City will create the opportunities for these students to have jobs to match their hopes and expectations remains to be seen. We, ourselves, find it difficult to imagine an immediate future for Newham in which sufficient new opportunities will be generated to meet the demand for locally-based work.

A multicultural society

Newham has a long history of cultural diversity dating back to the eighteenth century when Irish and Scottish farm labourers came to settle, looking for work in the market gardening areas and, later, as industry grew, as building labourers and construction workers. In the 1870s, the Irish were followed by German workers and Eastern Europeans – many of whom were Jews escaping from the pogroms – but many came simply to avoid the grinding poverty in their countries of origin.

In the 1911 Census, Newham, of all the outer London Boroughs,

13

had the largest number of 'immigrants' although in West Ham they made up only 1.5 per cent of the population and in East Ham 1.9 per cent. These figures were not solely the result of migration from Europe: they include 143 Asian seamen living in East Ham; and the Docks inevitably attracted a population from much further afield so that, by 1935, about 100 black families were living in Canning Town in addition to the sailors in hostel accommodation which made it the largest black community in London at the time. However, gradual dispersal and the bombing of Canning Town during World War II meant that this community left the area for good. During the 1930s and '60s wave of migration the black newcomers had to look for privately rented accommodation and this situation continued until the arrival of people expelled from East Africa in the late 1960s. Ironically this meant that the new council estates of Canning Town received few black people and this situation is still very much in evidence today.

Twenty-five per cent of Newham's population have their origins in the New Commonwealth or Pakistan. In North Forest Gate the figure was, until recently, 33 per cent (this percentage consisting of 55 per cent from the Indian sub-continent and 45 per cent of Afro-Caribbean origin). During 1986/7 there has been a large increase in the number of families from Bangladesh settling in the Borough. This has been the result of an established pattern of movement by successive groups from Whitechapel to Newham, and thence towards Essex, and partly the result of the provision of bed and breakfast accommodation for homeless families in Newham.

The daily experiences of recent settlers in Newham have often been troubled by fear of racial attacks on themselves or their children. Such attacks have been common and are regularly related to us by school students as well as appearing in the local press. Much animosity has been directed against the Asian communities particularly, it seems, by those established white communities which have suffered from the decline of manufacturing industry and the docks but this does not explain the wide-spread and deeply-rooted phenomenon of racism even among those who are better off. Recognizing this, the Borough has produced a policy framework for tackling racism and prejudice as part of a general policy to promote good race relations and equality of opportunity. (The Borough's Anti-Racist Short Statement is included as Document 8 in the Appendix.) Here too, as with employment prospects, students appear to be aware of the problems and see school as offering alternative possibilities.

> The fact that it is a multi-racial school helps to make one more
> aware of the different cultures in the world. Mixing with people

14

from other cultures has certainly broadened my horizons.

(Sixth former)

White people, black people, etc., can find out about each
others' cultures and this definitely aids relationships and breaks
down the colour barrier which is often seen outside the confines of
the school gates.

(Sixth former)

TABLE 2.1

Languages understood and/or spoken	Year 1	Year 2	Year 3	Year 4	Year 5
Panjabi	5	6	5	7	3
Gujerati	6	4	7	8	5
Urdu	2	1	4	3	3
Hindi	2	2	–	–	–
Bengali	9	9	17	23	12
Greek	–	–	1	1	–
Turkish	1	2	–	3	–
Cantonese	1	1	–	–	–
Panjabi Urdu	8	8	1	5	5
Gujerati Urdu	1	2	1	5	2
Panjabi Hindi	3	4	1	2	1
Panjabi Gujerati	2	1	–	1	–
Gujerati Hindi	7	1	4	5	2
Bengali Hindi	2	2	1	1	4
Bengali Urdu	3	–	–	1	–
Panjabi Gujerati Urdu	–	1	1	1	–
Panjabi Hindi Urdu	3	2	5	5	1
Panjabi Gujerati Hindi	–	1	3	4	–
Bengali Hindi Urdu	–	–	–	–	1
Gujerati Hindi Urdu	–	–	–	1	1
Panjabi Gujerati Hindi Urdu	–	–	–	1	3
Panjabi Bengali Hindi Urdu	–	–	–	1	–
Total	55	47	51	78	43
Total intake of students	131	130	146	180	175

N.B. The Survey form is included as Document 4 in the Appendix.

Schools are, we recognize, far from being havens set apart from the racial conflicts which characterize the rest of society but these students appear to have identified the importance of a school's acknowledgement that it is part of a multicultural society and committed to anti-racist policies.

It is of particular interest for the argument of this book that Forest Gate School has a population of students which is a microcosm of the linguistic diversity of the North Forest Gate area. This is mirrored in the languages and dialects which students know and use. Each year a survey of the linguistic abilities of the new intake of students is conducted and a break-down of the population of the school for the year 1986/7 in terms of home languages can be seen in Table 2.1. The Modern Languages Department has part-time teachers for Panjabi and Urdu and, as we report in later chapters, there have been substantial changes in the ways of working of the English as a Second Language (ESL) and Educational Support and Development (ESD) Departments to ensure that second language provision does not inadvertently obstruct second language learners' access to a full curriculum. At this point, it is only necessary to note that recognition of the linguistic backgrounds and skills of the students has been a key factor in bringing about changes in the curriculum and organization of the school.

Becoming a Community School

Since 1986 the school has been officially designated a Community School. This is the result of a long-term series of initiatives and negotiations beginning in 1980 with a residential staff conference.

> We were concerned that schools are often perceived as closed, unwelcoming bureaucracies and the aims we set ourselves were to open up the school, to make it a welcoming place to its pupils and the community, and to ensure that our curriculum reflected the community 'out there'.
>
> (Evaluation, July 1986)

This initiative by the school fitted closely with Newham's policy for community education in the borough. As stated by Leisha Fullick, chairperson of Newham Education Committee:

> We are trying to develop an educational service for the borough that is actually perceived to be relevant to the majority of the people here.
>
> (*The THES* 3.7.87)

On the ground, this has meant an emphasis on researching local needs and making, and keeping, contact with voluntary as well as statutory workers from the agencies and groups which are to be found in the community. Developing networks of contacts has been aided by the employment of an Outreach Teacher and the interest and goodwill generated by a Community Week in which the school students went out to find out more about the lives of the people in the area around the school and the school opened up its doors to invite in members of the community. This work has led to the development of a programme of activities which includes integrated daytime classes where adults, fifth and sixth formers study together; separate daytime classes where this is more appropriate (e.g. English as a Second Language, Keep Fit) and evening classes where there is a strong emphasis on new skills (e.g. computing), and leisure activities.

One result of these initiatives has been to bring a new body of students into the school. These are predominantly women who wish to further their education and enjoy recreational facilities while their young children are cared for in a full-time crèche. This provision is a key feature in these developments.

The policy statement produced by the school and which provides the basis for the work of the Community Council, established in October 1986 to plan the general direction of the community programme, is as follows:

Forest Gate Community School Policy Statement

We endorse the London Borough of Newham's commitment to achieving equality in education and employment in the Newham Education Service.

Students, staff, parents, and our community as a whole are expected to work together in expressing a positive and committed approach to encouraging respect for all individuals, races, and nationalities.

The curriculum, structures, and strategies of our community school must enable each student to reach the maximum of his/her potential.

We aim:

1. To give open and wide access to the curriculum, supporting individually and in groups those who have special needs in such a way that doors to learning are kept open, and there is no segregation.

17

2. To create an atmosphere of mutual support and respect which enables learning to take place effectively.
3. To encourage, especially through our Social Education programme, the acceptance of 'difference'.
4. To monitor and encourage good practice in pastoral and academic activities.

All staff should familiarize themselves with the London Borough of Newham's anti-racist statement and guidelines, noting that we are expected to carry out the policy described.

Incidents of racist or sexist behaviour should first be dealt with by the teacher who encounters it. It should then be reported to the Head of Year who will also deal with the matter, referring it to the Headteacher. A sub-committee of the Governing Body will monitor and recommend action on such incidents.

It is, however, recognized that such matters require more than disciplinary sanctions; counselling and follow-up are essential.

Our growth and development as individuals and as a community are dependent on our mutual respect and support.

As can be seen, the combined intention of school and borough have both symbolic and practical consequences. On the one hand, the school is making a public statement of its openness to the community it serves and acknowledges the diversity, and difficulty, that the word community represents. On the other, it has taken a number of practical steps to ensure that the school is a community school in more than name by opening up access to the school's resources, going out to make contacts, and encouraging a return to learning by adults whose needs have been ascertained. Perhaps most noticeable is the way in which 'becoming a community school' is seen, not as the addition of a parallel set of community activities to the mainstream curriculum, but one which has implications for the existing mainstream curriculum and the school's ethos and pastoral arrangements.

The current intake of first-year students comes predominantly from three local primary schools, with whom there are close links, with small numbers coming from further away. These 130 students are divided into five groups on entry and taught, usually in these mixed-ability groups, for the first three years. Maths is setted at the beginning of the third year and English remains in mixed ability groups in the fourth and fifth years.

The fourth-year curriculum provides a core of English, maths, social education and PE, which takes up 50 per cent of the timetable, whilst five option choices provide the other ten 65-minute lessons.

Pastoral continuity is maintained by form-tutors, as far as possible following their forms through their school career, whilst Year Heads coordinate the pastoral work for their own year. The sixth form works on the open-access principle referred to above. Of about 100 school students roughly 30 per cent are studying for A levels, the remainder taking a variety of one-year courses most of which are organized within the CPVE framework. Adult students attending day-time classes numbered 40 in 1986-7.

From what they say there is evidence that the first generation of adult students see themselves as part of a school community which values diversity of background and different levels of experience in its students. The following two quotations from *Forest Gate Community News* support such a statement:

> Since beginning 'Fresh Start' I have found that I learnt more in school than I thought I had, and that confidence was the factor lacking. Working together with women in the same situation is reassuring. Our problems with writing the English language are different, so we feel equally able to work with each other. The class teacher gives an added incentive in providing examples of the achievements of women who were in very much the same position as ourselves.

> I am a housewife with four children aged between seventeen and seven years old. I also do a part-time cleaning job. Community schooling is a boon to me, as it fits in with my other commitments. I do an English class three times a week with sixth-form students. I found it very strange the first time I attended class, but soon found that the students were ready to accept me. We get on well and I think we are a help to each other. For example, they can help me with the new teaching techniques and their fresh ideas, and I can help them with my experience of life and bringing up my own children.

We are aware that cynics may argue that schools polish up their image as caring communities in direct relationship to decline in school-age population; and open up their courses to adults for similar reasons. However, we think it only fair to record that, in our admittedly biased view, these changes in perspective and presentation have come about as a result of principled discussion and not opportunism.

Rumour and reputation

- Before I came to this school I didn't have any hopes – only fears and worries. You see I was only small and this school looked like prison every time I passed it and everyone (to me) looked so miserable. I was told stories of how you would get the cane if you didn't know your 19 times table by heart or on your birthday you got your head flushed down the toilet. Me, not being too brave, believed them and got scared. So overall before I came here I had a grim picture of Forest Gate School. I didn't have a clue what O levels were so school was a waste of time to me!

Now I've come here my views have changed (and I got a lot bigger so I got braver). The teachers are not (all) monsters and life at school 'ain't bad.

(Fourth year)

- I think it's very important to have a strict school and good education because we've got to think of our future as well.

  Most of the teachers are very nice and kind and they help you if you need help and they can control the class and they teach very good.

(First year)

- The school overall is a pleasant place to learn in. If I ever had to move anywhere around Newham I would still go to Forest Gate because of its general atmosphere.

(First year)

- People who live near our school don't really like us school-kids because we make a lot of noise at dinner time.

(First year)

- Forest Gate School seems to be a very good school. Although it may at times have received some bad publicity the teachers seem to be very dedicated.

(Sixth year)

- When I was coming to this school people frightened me with stories: when I came here there was no such thing as I was told.

(First year)

What matters most about a school? From the evidence in the comments quoted above, we suggest that what most concerns prospective students, and perhaps their parents, is the quality of the day-to-day encounters they will face. Will the new school be a place where they are scared, or will it be 'a pleasant place to learn in'? What matters to those already there, appears to be well-run classes where exam results can be achieved, together with a good 'general atmosphere'. For local residents and shopkeepers, or so we might guess by reading between the lines, it is how a school's students behave in the lunch hour, and at home times, that matters most of all.

Wherever they are situated, schools are involved in a similar set of tensions between rumour, reputation and reality. On the one hand, there are the school's public statements of aims, ideals, and expectations for its students; the ideal school hoped for by students, parents, teachers, governors, and local councils alike. On the other, there is the extent to which the 'scare' stories told to local primary age children and their parents about what goes on in a secondary school; the complaints from local shopkeepers; and the more widely distributed 'scare' stories in the local press are thought plausible and damaging.

Readers with close knowledge of secondary schools will have recognized that Forest Gate Community School is unexceptional. What the teachers, administration, ancillary workers, and support services set out to do are typical of the aims and intentions of their counterparts elsewhere in all kinds of rather different situations. The obstacles, difficulties and the success achieved – however this can be measured – are generally similar also. More difficult to judge, of course, is the importance of some of the less easily defined elements which appear to make schools, staff rooms and classrooms good (or otherwise) places to work in: generous relationships; positive attitudes to children and young people; good humour; flexibility; optimism. Forest Gate Community School has its clashes of ideas and interests, its outbursts of gloom, or anger, just like other schools. And it makes mistakes in failing to respond, or responding inappropriately, to community needs. We do, however, consider that, despite the fact that the school has not in any way been isolated from the economic and political factors which have affected schools generally (discussed more fully in the concluding chapters), it is remarkable that so many of the teaching staff have, as elsewhere, been willing to maintain an interest in curriculum development and in particular have been willing to put a considerable amount of time and intellectual energy into discussion of the effectiveness of the children's learning and it is to the story of that enterprise that we now turn.

Chapter 3

Getting started
John Hickman and Keith Kimberley

Much of the discussion in this and succeeding chapters centres round the work of a committee set up in 1981 to develop ideas and practices connected with language and learning. It was at that time one of a series of measures which were intended to establish regular discussion, review and development of aspects of school life. It took place alongside regular staff meetings; combined Head of Department and Head of Year meetings; and varying school-based, in-service initiatives. These included work on reading and readability, multicultural education, and mixed-ability teaching.

We think it is important to mention that the idea of a Language and Learning Committee was not new. As indicated in Chapter 1, work done in the late 1960s under the banner of Language Across the Curriculum had gained national recognition in *A Language for Life*, better known as the Bullock Report, (DE Science, 1975). In particular, Chapter 20 had included the proposals that *all* schools should have a policy to ensure that the role of language in learning be considered across all subjects and that a teacher, at a senior level, should be given responsibility for the development of such a programme.

Forest Gate Language and Learning Committee should be seen against these national perspectives and in relation to work already undertaken in the School in response to the Bullock Report. A committee had been set up in 1976 to follow up the Report's recommendation that schools should have 'a systematic reading programme for all ages'. Chaired by the Head of Maths and consisting mainly of heads of department (almost all departments being represented) it met regularly between March and June and its minutes show that its discussions ranged over a wide spectrum of educational issues. However, though points were raised on such themes as talk in the classroom; the language of teachers, of textbooks and of worksheets; dialect, accent and Standard English; testing; vocabulary lists and staff development, the Committee gave itself the title of 'The Reading Working Party' and eventually produced a report in June 1976 which was concerned with reading and the role of the Remedial Department. It made a number of proposals which involved additional staffing and resourcing for the Remedial Department, presented these to a staff meeting and was then disbanded – having fulfilled its brief. Thereafter a number of its recommendations were acted upon, mainly through and by the Remedial Department.

This approach seems to have been a common post-Bullock phenomenon: the setting up of a working party to produce a report or 'a policy'; the main effect of which was to displace longer-term processes of staff discussion and consultation, though, interestingly, a section of the minutes of the meeting of 25 March 1976 stated:

> One important consideration that should come from these discussions is the need for a forum for discussion among teachers of educational topics; and the importance of staff education.

A Language and Learning Committee

Five years later in the Language and Learning Committee we did in fact adopt an outlook very much in line with these sentiments. A meeting of representatives from all departments except one, convened by John Hickman as the senior teacher to whom the new headteacher had given responsibility for 'language across the curriculum,' concluded that:

1. The title 'Language across the Curriculum' would carry too much of the history, and perhaps stigma, of the mid-1970s when such committees seemed to proliferate, produce a document, and 'die'. 'Language and Learning' appeared to be a better description of the reason why all departments had an interest in coming together.
    (Not everyone was certain how much emphasis should be placed on *language*: part of the problem of the earlier committees in different schools had been a feeling that the English Department was trying to tell other people what to do – but everyone was convinced of the central importance of *learning* in all subjects.)
2. In order to discuss freely and openly some barriers between subject interests would have to be broken down. For this to happen it was agreed that there would have to be a sharing of information as to what went on in various subject areas. It was decided that, as a start, each representative would give an informal talk about the philosophy, policy and practice of his or her department.

23

3. There would be need for close attention to the membership of the Committee to ensure that it was representative of different levels of experience of teachers.
4. Communication between teachers across departmental divisions would need to be established and ways found of keeping everyone informed of, and involved in, initiatives.
5. The Committee should not impose a deadline on itself for the production of any report or policy. It should not restrict its interests to a restricted area of the curriculum; to a timescale; nor to any specific brief that it did not decide for itself. In other words, it should be seen as a permanent part of school life.

In retrospect, the Language and Learning Committee made several far-reaching decisions at that that first meeting. First, we set ourselves to explore processes rather than write a policy. Second, we realized that the Committee needed to be collaborative: that learning would have to be reciprocal between its members and transcend hierarchical relationships. Third, we recognized that a considerable effort would be needed if we were to develop methods of communication which crossed over the powerful boundaries which teachers set up around their subject interests. Fourth, we were proposing that our discussions about what, and how, students learn were a point around which school-wide professional development, affecting all teachers, should be based. Fifth, we had decided on a voluntary principle for attendance and agreed that meetings would take place outside timetabled time. A further feature of the arrangements, which will all be commented on further in later chapters, was our determination not to be bound by an agenda outside our control. This was seen as a key element in beginning to work together.

Two different kinds of presentation dominated our early work in the Committee. Representatives from art, religious education, maths, home economics, science, physical education, history, English, and geography departments reported on their work and interests. It became apparent that for some teachers the issues that were foremost in their minds were connected with explaining the nature of their subject and its organization, putting straight some long-standing myths. For others, key issues concerned the way school students work and how they interact in a specific classroom situation. Those who adopted the first approach appeared to feel that we all needed a baseline so that lack of knowledge of their subject's philosophy and practices didn't get in the way of discussion of language and learning implications. The latter were not uninterested in the special characteristics of their subjects but were particularly keen to start from the question of why school learning doesn't work for some students. And there were also two presentations which were cross-curricular in their focus. One, by a teacher with pastoral responsibilities, concerned issues of 'race and language' and another concerned support for second language teachers and students with learning difficulties. Both of these presentations, which are discussed in Chapter 4, sought to cut across subject preoccupations and challenged the group to consider whether there were broader perspectives for them to consider.

In retrospect, it seems to us that the terms of reference agreed at the very first meeting of the Committee were extremely influential in shaping our preoccupations later. We agreed to an exploratory year's work starting at a practical level with a look at what went on in our subjects. It was hoped that the committee would become a vehicle for interdepartmental discussion with regular statements of progress being made, perhaps at staff meetings. At our most ambitious, we hoped to build an understanding of the process of learning which would explore the relationship between our students and the curriculum we provide. We were interested in any theories which related to our work but we were primarily concerned to engage in our own research; to examine our own curriculum; and to see what changes we might wish to bring about in our own practice.

It also seems to us now that the kinds of questions it was decided to ask about classroom processes formed an agenda which persisted across a number of years. These questions concerned the balance of teacher, group, and individual talk as part of learning; opportunities for talk in relation to the task in hand and for chat; the amount and nature of writing required; and the extent of the students' interest in the curriculum.

Art

First to open up her subject, and thus her classroom, to the others in the group was an art teacher, Erika Shaw, who found herself patiently answering questions about what art teachers attempt to do. Some of this discussion later became part of a more formal presentation which is included as Chapter 5. Our interest in what art teachers expect from their students instantly took precedence over language issues and we learned in this first session just how narrowly prescribed our individual subject training had been. It became clear to us that our relationships to each other, especially the way we regarded each other's expertise, was likely to change as we were successively let into specialist knowledge of a kind not generally available, though not deliberately kept secret.

Religious Education

The discussion of the teaching of religious education which followed was fairly evenly divided between discussion of the RE department's syllabus and discussion by Ted Henderson of his own classroom procedures. As with art, there was a great deal to be learned about the nature of RE as a subject taught in school. The syllabus had recently been criticized by HMI as too unrelated to the pupils' previous experience and as making unreasonable conceptual demands, in particular on the first years. The department had agreed that their overall aim, which was to develop an awareness of the growth of religious belief and to understand the effect of that belief on people's lives, was probably difficult to fit together from some of the diverse elements which they had in the three-year course. This started from pre-history and the human search for meaning for first years and 'progressed', as students moved through into the second and third years, to religious leaders, world faiths, and how belief affects individuals.

The RE teachers had decided on a major reshaping of their course and had begun rewriting the first-year syllabus, starting from the diversity of experience which the children themselves could bring to the course. By centring the content around the conceptual framework of 'religion in the home' it was hoped that it would be possible to draw on the students' knowledge so that Jewish, Hindu, Sikh, Muslim and Christian students would all be able to relate to a particular part of the course and contribute their own experiences to the overall experience of each teaching group. Changes in years two and three were to follow.

Because Ted Henderson was willing to reflect on the range of language activities which occur in RE lessons and to be honest about the extent of teacher domination in most of them, he placed firmly on our agenda some major issues. By asking himself in public about the learning which was, or was not, taking place in his lessons, he articulated key paradoxes which face most teachers. How do you get talk in the classroom in which students grasp and develop concepts without imposing teacher views and knowledge? How do you get an orderly classroom without an excess of formality? How do you get a wide range of reading and writing activities to take place without undue reliance on structured worksheets and standardized tasks?

Talk in the classroom

The lesson format is what I suppose may be termed formal: its beginning comes from me talking to the class, and it turns towards the pupils in a question-answer session. Reading aloud is sometimes done from a textbook. Audio-visual material is used on occasion. The pupils are usually sitting in a formal arrangement: this reduces movement around the class and I suppose brings some element of order and discipline into the classroom. There are occasional questions through which I attempt to draw out particular points 'tying the knots' together, dotting the 'i's, and crossing the 't's. If I think there is an interesting idea within the reading then I usually bring it up for discussion. (My comments here are based on third-year work which I must admit is very knowledge-centred; lots of facts I feel have to be put across owing to the time pressure – after year three we no longer see the majority of pupils.)

In one sense I believe we are 'imposing' on the pupils more than we should. Fortunately, the change in syllabus will, I think, introduce a lot more new ideas in the school, though three years is still an inadequate amount of time for the subject.

Reading in the classroom

Beginning in year one, an understanding of the worksheet which is set is always necessary for the pupil to be able to do the work since the lesson is centred round the worksheet. The pupil needs to learn how to pick out the essential information as it is read through or referred back to during the lesson. Most of the work is based around worksheets which are used in conjunction with a particular textbook; one which covers the same material in more depth than the worksheet. The possible use of fiction is being considered to see whether it could stimulate the pupil to think about the significance and purpose of religious beliefs in certain situations.

Writing in the classroom

In all three years quite a proportion of the writing done is of the question-answer type although now in year one some questions allow greater flexibility, in the sense that pupils' own experience can be drawn into the answer and there are some wider possibilities in years two and three. Other writing activities undertaken are the reading together of a short passage which requires the pupils to write down the main points, and expressive work in which they are asked to place themselves imaginatively in a certain situation, using facts learned to provide the context and ideas.

In this session we were made aware of two related processes at work: one in which a major reappraisal of RE syllabus content was being undertaken in response to changing perceptions of students' backgrounds and experience and one in which some traditional assumptions about ways of teaching were being questioned. Each appeared to reinforce the other and to open up areas of discussion which continued to be issues through the history of the Language and Learning Committee.

Home Economics

The home economics teacher, Bernice Adkins, was, by contrast, more concerned with a backlog of staffroom misconceptions – and had perhaps some over-worn jokes to counteract.

Home Economics is not just another name for what was once domestic training for girls; it is not synonymous with Domestic Science or Housecraft but reflects a very different philosophy. Ours is not entirely an applied science subject and neither is it craft. The crafts of cookery, needlework and home-making remain important but the development of skills in these areas is no longer all that we are aiming for.

Definitions of Home Economics abound as we struggle for academic respectability and, more importantly, to justify our existence in educational terms. The department at present uses the definition of HE as:

'The study of the household group – its members' needs, values and relationships; its organization and management of available resources, and its relationship with the community of which it is a part.'

The adoption of this definition has been useful in shifting the emphasis from means which tended to become ends in themselves. For example, HE is not about cookery but about satisfying human needs, one of which is the need for acceptable food of the appropriate quality and quantity, and cookery skills are just one important resource in this context (others being time, money, foods available, etc.). It is not about infant nutrition, clothing, child development, social services or productive use of leisure time, but any or all of these topics may serve to illustrate the changing needs of individuals. We aim to relate knowledge about food, nutrition, housing, textiles, health, money, etc. to needs, values and relationships, i.e., raise the issues of priorities.

Bernice Adkins also had a well-developed view to share of the role played by language in the evaluating, problem-solving and decision-making activities in which she wanted the students to engage. It now seems clear how our interpretation of what is involved in studying language in the classroom was widening with each session.

From the very beginning of their course, first years are asked to evaluate their own and each other's practical cookery or needlecraft in discussion at the end of each lesson. At first it tends to be merely a criticism of finished results or the stage reached so far (usually flattering) but the aim is to encourage talk about procedures in order to check and improve understanding.

She was able to measure her aims against her practice in terms of getting a balance between information giving and using information and the development of manipulative skills giving particular attention to the needs of 'weak' readers and writers.

For the first half of term work sheets are mainly pictorial and poor readers can manage well since written instructions are always explained verbally, teacher demonstrations are frequent, and the children are encouraged to help each other. However, in the second half of the food studies course, there is a strong emphasis on group work in planning, organization, investigations and comparisons which relies heavily on written work. The only way in which poor writers can be helped is by placing them in groups, or pairs, in which someone else is always responsible for recording the plans, writing up assessments or conclusions after practical work, and reporting back to the whole class. Obviously, this is not satisfactory and the use of cassette recorders, if they were available, would enable greater participation by children with reading or language difficulties.

It is, of course, not possible to give a full account of a presentation and the discussion that followed it but two more ideas which emerged from this presentation may be considered worth including because they have recurred continually in the discussions of the Language and Learning Committee.

The first takes up the role of informal talk in the classroom. In the following comments the emphasis is mainly on the informal talk that relates to the task in hand but the occurrence of 'free' informal talk is observed and acknowledged. (Later we will refer to work by the Committee which examined more closely what goes on in 'free' informal talk.)

There is less time for informal talk during practical lessons than might be imagined. Very often it is important that discussion is restricted to talk about the task in hand since lack of concentration slows down the work and we are constantly aware of the very limited amount of HE time available for those pupils who do not opt for one of our courses in the fourth year. Most of the 'free', informal talk takes place during tasks that have become routine; probably only while clearing up for lower school students.

The second idea took the form of a suggestion by two of the HE teachers that their practice of observing each other in order to bring to light good and bad practices should be extended to 'all willing members of a department'; which almost certainly later helped to make it easier for other people to accept visitors to their lessons. As they then said, 'we expect it to contribute to renewal of the curriculum in the lower school.'

Successive presentations on maths, PE, history, science and English were not fully documented at the time and in our view this lower level of formality possibly helped us to be more relaxed with each other. It is not always easy to make explicit to other, perhaps critical, teachers how we teach, and why. (The maths presentation was written up later in a modified form and appears here as Chapter 6. The English presentation provided the basis for Chapter 7.)

Geography

One which was fully documented at the time was geography. Keith Mears' presentation was interesting, we think, because it combined teacher as expert; explaining the present state of thinking about the subject of geography with an interest in the dynamics of the classroom and what sort of sense the subject as taught made to the students.

Many geographers share a passionate (some might claim almost pathological!) concern about the philosophy and methodology of the discipline. No one approach dominates the Geography course at Forest Gate. There are elements of spatial organization, areal differentiation and ecosystems paradigms.

(*The Geography Curriculum*, Forest Gate School)

Perhaps for the first time we began to see something of the

students' point of view and what they have to do in order to make sense of the subjects which make use of terms and concepts not available in everyday language.

> Our syllabus, because of its choice of skills and concepts (from the concrete vernacular to the abstract technical), hopefully ensures that every child completes the core of the course which in turn then acts as a springboard to the work in the second year. It makes allowance for the effects of the six weeks' break; starts from the child's experience, scale being increased only gradually; confronts him or her with new experiences; involves simple problem-solving and decision-making as well as making direct use of the world beyond the confines of the classroom. Success and a growing confidence are intended to be integral outcomes of the activities. For some pupils success may appear guaranteed for little input of effort yet experience so far suggests that there is ample scope for challenging the most able via self-directed mapping tasks, the use of the computer and written and oral assignments.

> (*The Geography Curriculum*, Forest Gate School 5.3)

Also well established within the thinking of the Geography Department was a choice of options available to them in terms of teaching styles. The three models which were known to them and used in their planning of classroom activities are shown in Fig. 3.1. Keith Mears acknowledged that the methods of teaching used tended to be dominated by 'transmission-reception' and 'behaviour-shaping' models and that mixed ability grouping presented a considerable challenge to these. As part of the presentation, he offered a personal account of what happened in a short sequence from a 'typical' geography lesson.

What did the pupils actually do?

Second-year Geography. Tuesday periods 3 and 4. The class engaged in an exercise from a textbook on the classification of industry in San Francisco. They have been reminded of a long-term homework assignment. On the board is a list of instructions for the morning's work to reinforce my earlier verbal explanation.

Time: 11.10-11.20 a.m.
Pupil S is seated at the back of the room.
S: 'What am I going to write with?'
To T: 'Have you got to copy that?'
L then grabs for book. S gets up and comes out. Girl stands on his foot. S collects book and returns, limping. Glances at instructions

Figure 3.1 *Teaching-learning relationships*

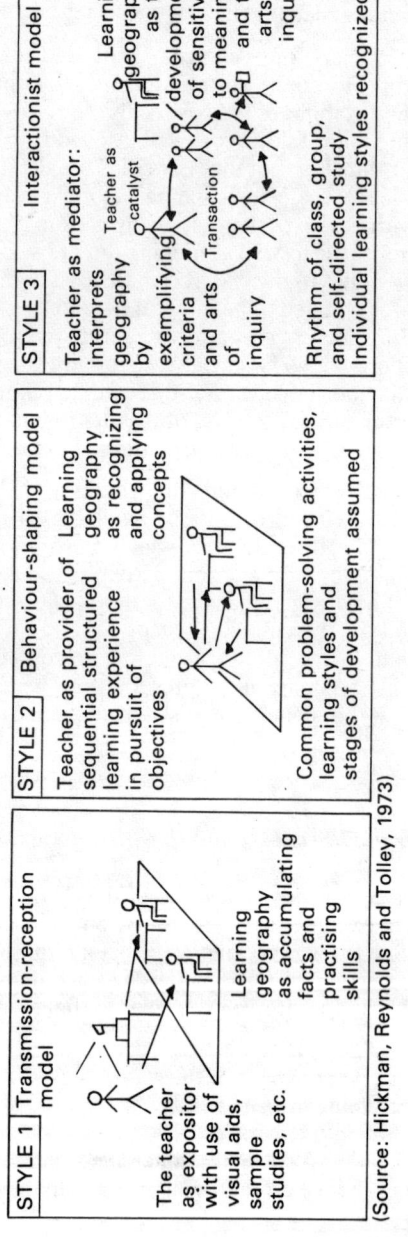

STYLE 1 Transmission-reception model

The teacher as expositor with use of visual aids, sample studies, etc.

Learning geography as accumulating facts and practising skills

STYLE 2 Behaviour-shaping model

Teacher as provider of sequential structured learning experience in pursuit of objectives

Learning geography as recognizing and applying concepts

Common problem-solving activities, learning styles and stages of development assumed

STYLE 3 Interactionist model

Teacher as mediator: interprets geography by exemplifying criteria and arts of inquiry

Teacher as catalyst

Transaction

Learning geography as the development of sensitivity to meanings and the arts of inquiry

Rhythm of class, group, and self-directed study
Individual learning styles recognized

(Source: Hickman, Reynolds and Tolley, 1973)

on board. Asks me for clarification. L grabs his book again. S: 'Sir, haven't I just got his book?' Argument ensues until I intervene. S looks round. Leans back on chair then gets up and walks around the room asking for a pencil. Returns to seat disappointed. Sorts out his paper earlier borrowed from me. S helps T with spelling. S looks at his own work and slaps desk. First removes a hair from his tongue and starts to trace (not part of the exercise). Leans back on chair. Looks at magazine on his lap. Carries on tracing. Leans back and looks at magazine again. Looks at T and spells word for him. Gives up tracing and draws or writes this time. This lasts 30 secs. Leans back for 5 secs and continues. Answers question from T. Leans back. Looks at mag. I at last give in and tell him off. After 15 secs S begins to gossip. Works for 50 secs. He then asks what to do next. Leans back and starts to read. Straightens papers and continues reading. Sees me glancing at him so he sits on the magazine. Leans back on his chair and carries on reading the textbook. Looks up after 15 secs. Glances down, looks up, glances down, looks up . . . yawns. Talks to T. Grimaces at L. Disturbed by T. Looks around then carries on reading. Yawns. . . .

Time: 11.22-11.32 a.m.
E uses pen as a guide in counting industries from the list. Uses rough paper to keep a tally. Says something to M. (I think she, E, is doing wrong questions!) Reads softly to herself. Screws up eyes, thinking hard (?). Scratches ear. Looks up. Turns back a page. Blows nose while still counting industries. Works very rapidly now. (11.26) Answers J's question. Explains her English homework. (Why are they doing English in my lesson and why are they doing geography in English?) M joins in. E's pen falls on floor. Someone returns a pencil to E. E blows nose while still counting and making rough notes. Checks her work (11.29). E sneezes. Looks at instructions on board. Gets up, returns book to cupboard and collects a new textbook. Says nothing. Sits down and turns to the page. Shows M. E borrows back her set square. E slackens M's tie. Smiles. Get on with work. Looks round at others gossiping. Carries on with work. (What a star!)

In providing material for close, if informal, analysis of classroom interaction, Keith Mears set a trend which others found it useful to follow through, using different techniques and investigating other teaching styles – in particular Model 3. It was a theme which was also included in the presentation on English. Though Elaine Mount talks from the teacher's perspective, she placed a great deal of stress on the importance of starting from the students' own experiences and knowledge and enabling them to take control of their own learning. How students can become autonomous learners in mixed-ability classes has continued to preoccupy the members of the Committee in their succeeding work.

This first sequence of presentations had, as can be seen from the fragments put together here, an important function in setting agendas, in establishing possibilities for future investigations and in alerting us to the wider social and theoretical issues that lie behind the decisions that teachers make about their subjects. The group had begun to relate differently to each other, developing some sense of trust that while their accounts of practice might be criticized they would also receive support from each other. Centrally, interest in each other's work and in the key issue of what sense students make of the experiences they are offered had developed both incrementally and with some unexpected leaps and bounds.

Chapter 4

Wider perspectives

John Hickman and Keith Kimberley

In the previous chapter we described some of the elements which made up the early work of the Language and Learning Committee. Towards the end of this sequence of presentations were three which, as we said earlier, pushed beyond the limits of subject concerns. One concerned language and race, another second language learning, and a third reported on a student's-eye view of a school day.

Contributing less as a history teacher than as someone interested in the whole curriculum and in the pastoral side of the School, Jon McGill presented a paper which opened up wide political debates about education. It would not be unfair to say that his paper covered so many different aspects of language and race in a short space (pidgin, creoles, bilingualism, second language learning, Standard English) that it perhaps confused as much as it elucidated. However, it very clearly established that there was a great deal of accurate linguistic information which teachers needed and that debates in the USA and the UK about language were of interest to teachers. It established that issues of race were not distant matters to be left to Rampton, and later Swann, (DES 1981, 1985) but had immediate practical implications for what was said and done in Newham – and by the Language and Learning Committee in particular.

> Standardization and the resultant failure of many children to live up to it, is an ideological tool which aids social separation, provides yet another means by which society is divided into competing groups with seemingly conflicting interests. Language teachers of all descriptions are often recruits in this ideology. In exacting certain kinds of linguistic standards from children with their own 'speech' we add, too, to the potential for racial division. Clearly, especially in the USA dialect has been offered as evidence of intellectual inferiority. The same phenomenon features here, when 'interference' is ignored or written off and the concept of 'culture laden' tests is not explored. Then it becomes too easy to see linguistic difficulties as explainable by reference to intellect.

Fundamentally important for our purposes is the connection between teacher attitudes and educational success. Two studies, one in Canada among French-Canadians and one in the USA by Labov,[1] have indicated that all types of predictions about job prospects and 'life-chances' are regularly made on the sole criterion of linguistic 'skill'. One interesting feature of both studies was that the 'minority' groups were just as biased in evaluating speakers of their own dialects. They had absorbed the mainstream prejudice. Another survey of West Indian-origin youth by Hebdige (1976) gives some evidence that Creole is on the rise as a means of resisting assimilation and 'preventing infiltration by the dominant group'. This indicates a worrying trend, if it strengthens the alienation of black youth from the 'standard' around them, thereby feeding strong stereotypes already in place.

When the focus shifts to 'Asian' pupils, the major difficulties revolve around whether universally accepted languages, with deep historical and linguistic roots, can be somehow incorporated into school experiences for the non-English speaking child. The Mother-tongue debate raises issues of both racial nonacceptance and of the intractability of school curricula. However, at present we clearly strip Asian children of the security offered by their own language.

My own leaning is toward incorporation of the child who is learning English as a second language into a more normal school day, without the stigmatization of withdrawal or special grouping. This calls into question not only foreign language teaching but the nature, too, of the teaching of reading in general. There must be deep linkage between inadequate theories of reading for the English-speaking child and the non-English speaker. Similar methods are often used for both, with results which leave many children out in the linguistic cold. When added to this picture, the factor of 'cannot speak English, thus cannot think' becomes crucial.

This presentation reminded us that research is not neutral and that opened out the discussion into areas where research findings are contested. The basic assumption on which some policies are based were called in question and Jon McGill focused on specific details of language use (description of some of the features of English-based West Indian Creole dialect formed a significant section of the paper). He made no claim to expertise: this he argued was an investigation of the issues. As he himself said,

I make no prescriptions where language is concerned, since I have neither the expertise in linguistics nor 'practice' in dialect.

Nevertheless, it is pointless to abdicate the responsibility of suggesting how we might better inform ourselves, how we might be more aware of the interference of our own prejudices or standards in the education of all children and specifically, black children. I argue, therefore, for a concrete role in schools for dialect. This can be done and has been done in many areas. However, there are specific problems, not least teacher and pupil attitudes. In particular, the child will avoid exposing his/her language to possible ridicule or 'research'. Some West Indian origin children disclaim knowledge of Creole. How Creole is used in schools is less important than the welcome it receives as a valid linguistic tool. That welcome is then dependent upon teacher education in the nuances of not only Creole but the culture which produced it. Seen in this light, dialect becomes much more than something 'sing-song' or pleasant to the ear. It emerges as validation of black presence in English schools.

Of course, language is but one feature of the 'problem' of race for, and in, British schools. Problem it most definitely is, but it is a functional and institutional problem lying inside the school system not within the pupils or the ubiquitous cited 'home backgrounds' or in 'cultural deprivation'. The main deprivation in this context is of access, respect, and the lack of a sense of adventure in pursuing the new which is found amongst the teaching profession in general. I have left aside, in this paper, the issue of racism inside the language; this should be taken up at a later date. It is an issue given little attention. In general, it is suggested that we examine texts and materials, which is fine. However, too often linguists shrug off the effects of racialism implicit in language. The language, as a social construct, reflects social values and attitudes, and it would be a rare language indeed which, in a racist society, did not reinforce and reflect that value in itself.

A presentation of this kind had a number of significant consequences for the Language and Learning Committee. It strengthened a tendency, already introduced by others in one or two of the earlier presentations, that it was appropriate to look outside the school for ideas, for example from academic fields such as sociology, curriculum studies, or sociolinguistics, and also to examine official reports, surveys and policy documents on education for items of relevance to their concerns. It also reminded us that though we might start discussing certain issues in terms of classroom practice they were also located in much wider political frameworks which we would be unable to ignore.

In retrospect we can see that some of Jon McGill's arguments needed more careful clarification and that writing today he would be likely to give a different emphasis in some places. However, we think it is important to show the value we found when individual teachers were willing to try out on us ideas from their reading and discussions outside school.

Many of the issues he raised were to reverberate through the thinking of the group and to reappear in other formulations. It is also relevant to note that a presentation of statements on issues like Standard English, dialect, mother tongues, black resistance, testing, and racism inevitably generated counter argument and discussion. Increasingly we found that contentious issues tended to niggle away at our consciousness outside as well as inside meetings, in informal situations as well as more formal ones.

Two other presentations which caused the Committee to think in a less subject-centred way were one on support for second language learners in the mainstream classroom given jointly by Maggie Farrar and Elaine Mount and one in which Nicki Regan gave an account of spending a day with a first-year class. These two presentations, given at the same meeting, appear to have had a major impact on the way in which the Committee was to use its time over the next two years. During the period that this book documents the nature of both Remedial and English as a Second Language provision in the School have undergone major structural and ideological changes. This is documented in Chapters 11, 13, and 14 which give accounts of the moves from thinking associated with separate departments to a support and advisory role within the mainstream curriculum. For both groups of 'specialists' the changes have meant a major reappraisal of their day-to-day work and thus, throughout the period, they have been in a special position with regards to discussion of language and learning. Since beginning to work alongside students in an increasing number of subjects across the curriculum, they have become freshly aware of the demands being made, and not made, on students and have been able to explore new forms of teaching partnership.

Nicki Regan's account of a day spent with a particular group of students meshed very closely with the preoccupations of the ESL and ESD teachers because of her determination to uncover the mismatch between what teachers think students are getting from their lessons and what they actually experience. In dredging through the notes from the meetings of this period, we discovered that initially five people said they were going to follow a class round and report in writing on their experiences and that a further five, perhaps with specific areas on which to concentrate, would then follow. In the event only one account saw the light of day – a reminder that such tasks make substantial demands on teachers' time and energy.

We think, again with hindsight, that it was through discussions which followed on from presentations like these that the part played by talk in learning began to be displaced a little in favour of writing and reading. In part this shift of attention corresponds to changes taking place nationally and internationally from the spoken to the written. Within the school, people were beginning to suggest that the difficulty our students had with some of the tasks given them often related to the nature of the writing required and the difficulty of the texts to be read. Three INSET (In-Service Education of Teachers) sessions provided for the whole staff on the readability of texts, were fed into our discussions at this point and it was suggested that we should make the books and work sheets used at Forest Gate one of our prime concerns. A parallel suggestion was that it would be useful to look at writing in specific curriculum areas. Together with the continuing work on talk and learning, it is easy to see now how the Committee was starting to move into a new pattern of working with sub-groups pursuing different lines of inquiry.

As can be seen, this was a time of considerable excitement of everyone involved. Keith Mears brought in some suggestions for classroom observation from the Open University Course 'Curriculum in Action' which required only a notebook and some relatively small amounts of time, but there was also talk of making tape recordings, of using video, and of reading articles or books for a series of seminars. Notes from a meeting considering the way forward include the following summary of the way we then saw our situation.

There are two issues to consider:

1.   How can the Committee proceed so that individuals on it can:

    (a)   most effectively examine their own practice?
    (b)   most profitably explore new ideas and other people's philosophy?
    (c)   most positively use and share their own talents and insights?
    (d)   most effectively develop their own thinking and pedagogy?

These points have to be taken up without people feeling that the Committee is taking up a disproportionate amount of their time.

2.   How can the Committee most effectively communicate with the rest of the staff so that:

    (a)   the issues discussed have a wider audience?
    (b)   ideas generated have the potential to be converted into the hard currency of school policy and curriculum development?

Behind the clouds of optimism there is here an indication of the dilemmas we were then experiencing. Rewarding as people were finding the discussions and studies they were undertaking, it was still work additional to the day-to-day business of teaching. Additionally, the more idealistic and enthusiastic a group of people working voluntarily become about what they are doing the more likely it is that people not involved will begin to have, and express, reservations and negative feelings about the enterprise. We were aware of this beginning to happen and were to seek ways of avoiding it, with differing degrees of success, across the following months.

One of the initiatives proposed at this point to involve the whole staff was the holding of a staff meeting, or series of staff meetings, to share some of the work that had gone on in the Committee. On our part, we were convinced that what was happening in the group was a particularly effective form of school-based INSET by virtue of the continuing dialogue that was taking place. There was also pressure from the Head Teacher and other staff that the work of the Committee should feed back into the school at large; if members of the group were beginning to peep out from the safety of their subject cocoons and shed some of their traditional prejudices about other subject areas, it was surely time for there to be a wider sharing of these perspectives. In the event, for a variety of practical reasons, including a transport strike, the staff meeting did not take place.

It should be acknowledged that we did have some reservations both at this time, and later, about 'going public'. This stemmed from the view which we generally held about the ways in which relationships work in schools and the nature of the processes involved.

With respect to the former, the Committee was itself made up of representatives from across the whole curriculum and so thought that the most effective route for contributions to curriculum development was to get issues being discussed in the Language and Learning Committee onto department meeting agendas. This we hoped would avoid any sense of a self-righteous group telling colleagues how to teach. Similarly though we liked to think that members of the Committee would be well-equipped to contribute to whole-school in-service initiatives on such subjects as teaching mixed-ability groups, we felt that this would best be done within the school's general in-service planning rather than as initiatives from the Language and Learning Committee.

With respect to the latter, we were aware that the main emphasis of our work had been on processes and not products and that there was some danger both in the Committee and the school of generating the kind of frustration that mounts when one seems to be uncovering more questions than answers. The desire for neatly packaged solutions is strong in all of us but, if we were to continue to take on the complexities of language and learning, the desire would rarely, if ever, be fully satisfied. Given this, we were aware of the difficulties involved in putting moulds onto particular issues and making public statements. The way of working of the Committee, in which there was space and time for people to listen to 'strange' ideas and to readjust their thinking in a fairly relaxed and informal context, would be difficult to achieve in a wider forum.

There was, however, one way in which we thought contributions could be made which recognized the complexity of the processes involved and which could involve the Committee members as a group. This was to write up personal presentations and any classroom investigations for the rest of the staff. We did, of course, see some benefit to ourselves in writing down, and thereby having to make explicit, what had been perhaps loosely asserted or described. We also explored, and wrote an introduction (see Appendix Document 2) for a staff booklet on Talk and Learning. This did not materialize.

At the same time the group made two important decisions. One was to have a series of 'seminars' around articles or extracts on different aspects of language and learning. This grew from a perceived need to relate practical and theoretical perspectives and also from an increasing involvement of members of the group on diploma and MA courses. The other was to set up sub-committees to pursue particular lines of inquiry. John Hickman as chairperson/secretary to the Committee suggested that, on the basis of the interests people had so far expressed, there might be groups on: talking and learning; writing across the curriculum; language development outside the English classroom; ESL in the mainstream classroom; and reading demands across the curriculum. These proposals became the focus for discussions at the beginning of the 1982-3 school year as a result of which gender and race in education was added to the list.

Because we thought that the kind of research being proposed might be interesting to a cross-section of the staff which went beyond the limits of the committee's membership, a circular was sent to all members of the teaching staff offering: active participation in the research groups: after-school in-service sessions for the presentation and discussion of findings; full staff meetings on specific topics; dissemination of written reports; availability of reading material on given topics; and outside speakers. The questionnaire was returned by 27 members of staff out of a possible total of 68. The information we received is set out as Table 4.1.

An examination of the inclinations of those who replied shows that they were broadly in favour of the work in hand and wanted to be kept informed of new ideas that might be around and to know of any outcomes from investigations being undertaken. We must also assume that those who did not reply had reservations about the work of the Committee or were disinclined to take on the extra demands

TABLE 4.1 *Language and Learning Questionnaire*

	I would like to participate actively in this group	I would attend an INSET session on this subject	I would like a staff meeting to be devoted to this subject	I would like to receive any reports or papers written by this group	I would like to receive any reading material that this group are studying	I would attend a film or a talk given by an outside speaker on this subject	I feel that this subject is irrelevant to my needs at the moment
1. Talk and Learning across the Curriculum	6	11	5	20	13	13	–
2. Writing in different subject areas	4	12	4	20	17	14	–
3. Language Development outside the specialist English Classroom	4	12	4	17	15	14	–
4. Gender and Race in Education	7	12	7	19	16	13	–
5. ESL in the Mainstream Classroom	3	6	8	20	16	15	–
6. Investigation of Reading demands across the Curriculum	3	17	7	17	15	13	–

which were being made on people's time and energies. The return also indicates that 17 people were willing to contribute actively to one or other of the investigations being proposed and that, while staff meetings received little support, written reports were thought particularly helpful.

So it was in January 1983 that three groups, Language Development outside the English Classroom, Gender and Race, and ESL in the Mainstream Classroom, began investigations which were to continue with varying degrees of commitment over the next year and a half. The successes and failures of these groups will be followed up in Chapter 11. Here we only wish to indicate the kind of questions groups intended to address. For example, the Language Development group were intent on answering such basic questions as what was meant by language development and considering how it might be most effectively monitored and assessed in different subject areas. They were interested in expressive uses of language and the potential of dramatic activity, as well as in the types of writing and reading required in different subjects. The Gender and Race group were concerned with how they could investigate bias and stereotyping in materials and classroom practice and wanted to find out whether there was evidence that girls were treated differently in Forest Gate classrooms from boys. They were particularly keen to see whether teachers' expectations were different in any ways between boys and girls or between Blacks, Asians and Whites. These groups had lists of books they intended to read in addition to their investigations, while, by contrast, the starting point of the ESL group was practice. They wished to see what they might learn about the school's present ESL provision, and to explore ways in which classroom teachers might be able to cope on a day-to-day basis more effectively. They hoped to explore the role of mother tongue in learning and end up being able to propose ideas for in-service sessions and the development of materials.

We have deliberately left out discussion of the Talk and Learning group up to this point because the pressures on this group were somewhat different and it seems worth discussing their involvement with groups outside the school. As we noted above, involvement in the kind of activity we have been describing in school tends to have a 'knock on' effect in encouraging people to go to courses, conferences, sign up for diploma or MA courses and so on. It conversely also appears to give people already committed to courses of educational study a way of feeding back ideas into their practice. A similar 'knock-on' effect worked for the Talk and Learning group in their relation to the Schools' Council Language for Learning Project.

An initiative had been taken by Jed Melia – the English Adviser for Newham – to involve the Borough's teachers in this project and a

Newham Advisory Teacher – Mark Cremin – was seconded in order to work with Jean Bleach, the Project Director, and to organize working groups within the Borough. Over a period of two years this resulted in a number of weekend conferences attended by primary teachers and secondary English/drama teachers. Both John Hickman and Dave Lewis from Forest Gate School became involved in this project.

Discussion of talk and learning was spiralling within the school and the Borough, encouraged and enhanced by the work of the Schools' Council Project. This complex network only really becomes clear in hindsight: there is not a logical, continuous thread to the activities and there was no controlling, organizing force. As so often happens in schools the seed of an initiative took on a will of its own and a momentum was built up which made connections in many areas.

The relationship with the Language for Learning Project had also a second strand through the English Department's involvement with the London Association for the Teaching of English (LATE). John Hickman had managed to persuade Erika Shaw and Tony Jones to give versions of their school presentations to a group of English teachers at a conference on Talk and Learning which LATE was running in association with the Schools Council Project. The group they spoke to were attentive, asked them difficult questions but left them in no doubt that what they had to say was interesting to others. In particular Tony Jones' analysis of his own teaching (Chapter 6) challenged the teachers of English to explain, and to some extent revise, their prejudices with respect to 'transmission' teaching and, conversely, caused him to go back and investigate further the importance of collaboration in maths learning. The LATE Conference had the effect of consolidating work that had begun in the Language and Learning Committee. It also drew teachers from Forest Gate into a LATE Working Party on Talk chaired by Keith Kimberley, which was later to become instrumental in generating this book. From the beginning this group, which met monthly, was, it must be confessed, dominated by the Forest Gate membership and concerns. Its connection with the Schools' Council Project provided further encouragement to investigate and write up. Thus the school's Talk and Learning Research group made use of the following guidelines which had been agreed by the LATE group for its work:

Talk and Learning

The following areas are tentative guidelines for the writing up of the Talk and Learning project.

Engagement

Under this heading we are asking you to look at those factors which encourage students to become involved in doing something or in thinking something through. You might wish to look at how they make the teacher's tasks their own; at whether collective activity is an important means of generating interest and energy in relation to task; at the degree of autonomy available to the students; at the effects of students having to formulate thoughts and speak in front of the whole class; of the importance of receptiveness and appreciation in the small working group.

Expectations

Under this heading might be included some analysis of students' expectations of the classroom activities and the subject taught. Examination of the sense of continuity shared by teacher and student might include running jokes, previous joint experiences, teacher expectation of what individuals or groups can achieve (alone, or with help), tacit understanding about content, activities, etc. The focus would be on the 'history' of the class and the teacher's shared experience.

Intellectual and emotional development

Under this heading you might examine the ways in which the intellectual progress of individuals, or groups, is monitored and the interventions which are made by the teacher as a result. You might wish to look at the problems involved in teacher intervention (!) in organizing the lesson; in interactions during the lesson with individuals, groups and the whole class; and in putting a framework onto the activities the students have been engaged at the end of the lesson. You might pay attention to the demands made on individuals by the others in small group discussion. Similarly, you might wish to look at how the teacher or other students contribute to extending the emotional perspectives of an activity. In particular, we are interested to know if there are important issues to do with cohesion and conflict in small groups of students learning together. For example, is a certain amount of abrasiveness necessary if a cosy consensus is to be avoided? Finally, you may want to reflect on where the main intellectual demands of your subject are made: through the books chosen for study, through the written work set, through talk in the nature of the task set, or at some other level.

All this may help the reader to interpret the next six chapters. Erika Shaw's chapter is derived from the first presentation and explores the kind of informal talk that is incidental to learning in the art classroom. Tony Jones, who gave the third presentation, by contrast is concerned with the teacher's role in structuring talk in a maths lesson. The chapters by Elaine Mount and Dave Lewis have as their main emphasis an attempt to relate the learning that goes on through talking, writing, and reading and show how they tried to explore ways in which teachers can assess and manage group talk. Jon McGill's chapter looks at different functions of talk, including drama and debate, within the history lesson and considers the tendency of teachers to inhibit students' learning. The final chapter in this section of the book is by a primary teacher who was drawn in to the activities of the LATE Talk Working Party through her involvement in Newham's Language for Learning Project and was able to contribute a different set of perspectives from those taken for granted by the secondary teachers.

NOTE

1 The Canadian studies referred to used the 'matched guise' techniques developed by Lambert and his associates in the 1960s. People were asked to attribute various traits to different samples of speech made by the same speakers using different languages, dialects, or accents. The studies by Labov were conducted in New York and focused on the way that differences in speech evoke standardized responses in listeners. For a helpful summary of the issues see Edwards (1976) pp. 16-30.

Part Two

Presentations and Investigations

Chapter 5
Talk in the art room
Erika Shaw

In this chapter Erika Shaw reflects on her own practice. Though she made a recording of talk in her lessons, she does not analyse this in detail but gives an art teacher's view of the ways in which she attempts to extend her students' ideas and perceptions through talking with them.

Art can be subjective, objective and experimental all at once (perhaps as all other subjects should be) – it is essentially a decision-making and selection-biased subject which also depends upon fortunate mistakes that can be recognized and built upon. The job of the teacher, as I see it, is in enabling adolescents to discriminate and understand the power of those choices open to them.

At around the age of eleven or so there appears to be a marked development in adolescents' self-consciousness. They are often especially self-critical of their creative work and urgently need to develop confidence in what they produce. Consequently, I think there are dangers in too rigidly controlling the form that work in art lessons should take lest form becomes an inhibiting, rather than an enabling factor. In the classroom I hope that I am continually encouraging their confidence, treating their insecurity almost as if it were a frontier to be conquered.

Actually, in relation to achieving this, I've got an uncomfortable feeling that I spend too much time talking about the wrong things, i.e. tidiness – use of paint – classroom procedures, but I also come to the lesson as a thinking, feeling person and I need a certain air of order and containment in the proceedings so that I can relax and feel able to give gentle but firm support to those who need it.

In terms of lesson talk I do not really discuss the problems in hand at great length for they do not actually exist until the children have made their own attempts. Also, they themselves have ideas and I am thankful for that, because twenty children all needing my personal attention would be difficult to orchestrate, and also because the advice and help they can give each other has immense value. My opinion may be followed because it is wise to do what Miss says – but pleasing the teacher does not necessarily lead to a good grasp of the problems faced. Also they are all struggling with similar problems – I, in my lofty status of having acquired and understood the knowledge, am often 'blind' to the problems they experience in the process of learning.

The presentation and content of the work to be carried out must be lively and imaginative whatever the level. Even the most simple painting methods and exercises in lower school need to be enticing to look at and often involve the presentation of step by step instruction and example. Each process in the whole exercise must be broken down into a set of logical and progressive basic tasks and along with the identification with these in a visual way there is usually the running commentary from the teacher whose language must echo the simplicity of the task, explaining and introducing specific technical or specialized terms where necessary. One presentation is never enough and the need to repeat and reclarify both by verbal and visual means is constant. The redefinition of a problem or task outside the art context, perhaps offering a parallel problem, can often be beneficial. If a boy is drawing a figure but is finding it difficult to assess and execute the correct gradient and direction of a particular line of the arm, the use of the eraser at this point does not lead to a correction. In fact, he is likely to draw the line back from where he has just removed it. I could show him and correct the line but there would, of course, be little learning in this. So I suggest he can leave the incorrect line in place and draw the correction alongside it. Usually there is a reluctance to do this as 'untidy' but a comparison with the use of scaffolding in building construction which enables the building to progress but is removed when no longer necessary can often persuade the pupil to do something which at first he abhors. He may then assess his new statement in conjunction with the old, adjust the angle and, once satisfied it is correct, remove the original mark.

The discussion of ideas is especially important in a subject heavily concerned with imagination. If I want to generate enthusiasm for an idea, I myself must emanate enthusiasm, by the way I paint a picture verbally and draw the group into the process of creation, constantly building up the confidence and motivation by describing, using many varied words and word associations and getting the group to spark off each other. Often at the introduction of a piece of creative work the groups of children involve themselves in lively discussion of their ideas and plans. This is very valuable. They test out theories and exchange stimuli and ideas and then, once satisfied with the potpourri of images, they begin the practical execution. This also involves asking me questions about technical processes and here a demonstration of the separate stages accompanied by a verbal account is useful. With older groups of pupils, it is useful to get them to write down a list of words associated with a topic or ask a set of questions around it. For them a one word topic or a title can spark off a multitude of ideas; but although the ideas may flow freely, the problem for the teacher often lies in the enabling process; that is the linking of the physical task of creating with hands to the intellectual development of the idea. The title 'Night-time' may benefit from a series of questions being asked to clarify the personal imagery which is resolving itself in individuals' minds.

1. Is it completely dark?
2. Where is the light coming from? – The decisions about the source are manifold: street lamp, torch, flame, shop window, car, lamp, moon, open doorway, etc.
3. From which angle or position do we view the scene – from above, the side, below – and to which degree in each direction?

With this method a host of possibilities – both mine and those of the pupils are hurled forth, building up personal responses to the simple, one word title – each result relying very much on the group's shared thinking.

Advice about how to produce an image and which medium to work in can be offered together with detailed technical advice (e.g. how viscous should the paint be or how to hold the brush for maximum control and manoeuvrability). Wonders can be achieved by pointing out that, unlike writing, you can paint upside down. At all times demonstration is the key to action but always accompanied by a verbal explanation that removes the mystique.

In art, the result of each individual's labours is immediately on show to his or her neighbours – all is revealed as the creative process takes place. It is easily accessible to all onlookers and there is therefore usually some cross-referencing of ideas and opinions, welcome or otherwise, about progress. Ideas are exchanged: discussion about colour, tone, proportion, harmony, style; is the paint too thick or too thin? Has the paint been correctly aligned? Should I use pastels? Each individual is engaged in a continual filtering process taking on board only those ideas that are suitable, or can be adapted.

Often children seek the teacher's approval at regular intervals and, if there are no problems, a quick confirmation of what they are doing will lead to continuation. If there is a problem, a one-to-one discussion can be very effective. Sometimes the problem is widely spread amongst members of a group and it can be useful to stop and draw everyone's attention to how one particular pupil has pinpointed something we could all look out for.

As far as personal progress goes, it is often difficult to share my sense of pleasure in the kinds of achievement that I appreciate with a child who does not understand the finer nuances of what I am praising. The teacher can wax lyrical about a particular texture, or colour, or complementary shapes but to have the pupil see and understand and feel the success too, is another thing altogether. The child may be pleased to please his teacher but a true success is being pleased with the work itself. Success can be like a patchwork with similar sequences being re-emphasized and scattered over time rather than all apparent in one solid piece of work. Therefore it is important that the child is able to recognize these, as they occur, or is at least made aware of them throughout the network of responses the teacher makes. Verbal approval as well as display are all reinforcement towards this goal.

Within the artroom an atmosphere which is casual without being slack, and with room for light-hearted jokes and banter can facilitate a wider sense of group contact. The children often sit in the same place each week with friends and often tackle work in a similar way but also very often in order to discuss varied topics from areas not connected with their activity. I think this talk is important for, although at times it can be distracting and interfere with progress, it is also a way of tuning in to some part of the mind that releases the subconscious creative level so that this can flow freely whilst the conscious mind is 'occupied'. By contrast I also use the tactic of contradistinction, expecting total silence so that the conscious logical and rational elements of the task are given the upper hand. With this approach there are no distractions from the strong concentrated effort, and, although at first there is much resistance to this, once the results have been seen the children are usually pleasantly surprised to see for themselves how it has helped and are keen to do more. However, to actually describe this as true silence is misleading for I really mean that the pupils remain silent. I myself describe what it is they are drawing, point out what to look for; point out details they may not have observed for themselves, how to vary the way they use the pencil; and hope that somehow the words will be processed, and eventually flowing out in deeds upon the page – which does actually seem to happen.

Often it is those who at first seem to be having the greatest struggles who actually make the most progress. Natural talent can be a great asset but it can also result in laziness within the subject, so that a child may be able to produce a very satisfactory piece of work but does not really test or stretch himself; very often children fall back on those things they know they can do and consequently make very few moves forward. No intellectualization has occurred. A struggle often leads to more valid development and satisfaction.

Display is also an important part of the sequence, and not only for the best work. It is as a means of saying that someone has tried hard and that this has been recognized. The display attracts the attention of other pupils and they are eager to compare and contrast results and air their views and criticisms, to herald successes and also to say what they do not like. All this is important for it extends their responses to the visual stimuli around them and helps them to place their work into a wider context of achievement.

Efforts are rewarded even if attainment is not immediately obvious. The teacher's role of 'judge' has to be altered readily depending upon who is to be 'judged'. Some individuals need to be nurtured and have their fragile self-confidence bolstered and fortified by gentle but firm insistence that they complete a task instead of giving up yet again. Some people are good at starting anew but never finish. They shy away from the problem solving that is the nub of it all. This problem seems to worsen with older pupils whose expectations about themselves are very set, and often if their skills are not those that they would wish to have they prefer to produce nothing. Other pupils need to be helped constantly by the teacher and given assistance at many frequent stages, even when it comes to deciding about a choice of colour. This support can usually be given without actually doing the problem solving for them. Yet others need to be avoided as they rely heavily on teacher interference simply as a way of avoiding work themselves. Sometimes other members of the group are imposed upon in this way. Again a judgment must be made. One pupil helping another can be a very useful exercise for the teacher cannot always be where she is needed or when she is needed. The teacher can sometimes be too far removed by her skill to understand the simple problem and can actually be excluded by this from any real contact with some children who can actually feel more comfortable with a certain amount of assistance from a more able friend. The child being helped does not suffer from the stigma of always having to be shown again what to do. For the young assistant it is also a way in which she or he can reinforce what has been learned by having to find a way of passing it on to another.

Art is an extremely personal pursuit. In the end there can only be advice and gentle persuasion towards trying to stretch the rigid barriers that children erect around themselves. While some are able to do this for themselves, an equal number need all sorts of pushing, shoving, coaxing and flattery to get them there. But whoever you are – it is not good enough to simply go through the motions. If you easily produce good work from the most basic to the most highly advanced without a struggle but skirt around, or shy away from, solving a problem you are robbing the creative process of its intrinsic intellectual aspect.

The teacher has to try to give support (however active or passive) to all the individuals within a group at all times, however impossible it may seem. This means trying to talk in detail to all the students about his or her objectives, even if things appear to be unclear, discussion and gentle probing can clarify hazy ideas and notions, then enabling the results to be accepted or rejected and perhaps more importantly knowing why. This leads to a more rounded sense of achievement – even if the steps taken are only small, they hold more value and are a sturdier foundation for further development.

This, in an ideal situation, would mean one-to-one interaction, at leisure, but the real world of classroom teaching can only offer compromise; good planning and organization can potentially ease the strain. Anticipating problem areas before they arrive and explaining strategies to combat them in advance can help to release the teacher for more meaningful teacher/pupil talk. Each pupil's personal problem can then be tackled as it arrives whilst the rest continue by themselves. The individual is then free to engage the teacher or the teacher engage the individual about crucial struggles with the creative process. Hopefully this leads to an atmosphere where students can work by themselves and not feel restricted by the teacher's requirements of them, but also secure that if they should need it, advice is near at hand.

Talk is the major component of any teacher's repertoire and although demonstration is high on the list, verbal communication still rules supreme. The key to the talk problem is one of making sure that the talk remains relevant; that it does not overshadow the doing and always stays as a thoroughfare for learning.

Chapter 6

Teaching maths: the enthusiasm factor

Tony Jones

In this chapter, Tony Jones looks at the importance of enthusiasm and structure in the mathematics classroom. He admits to dominating the discourse both in terms of time and control. He argues that if the students accept his framework of classroom procedures, it provides the context in which both sequential thinking and intuitive leaps are possible.

Methods of systematically classifying the modes and functions of speech in the classroom are already well documented and much discussed, but the function of talk that I wish to emphasize is often played down or even ignored. It is the use of talk as a means of generating, communicating and inspiring enthusiasm. Enthusiasm is infectious if it is apparent and initially it may be expected to come from the teacher. Classify teachers you have known into those with either a cynical, disillusioned or bored attitude to their subject, and job, or with an insecure knowledge of their subject, and into those with a genuine enthusiasm for their subject, those who are constantly reviewing and updating their approach; then observe their classes. The enthusiastic teacher will exude enthusiasm through every sentence he or she utters to the class and this is the prime importance of teacher talk, in my view.

The examples I cite during the rest of this article pertain to a third-year top mathematics set. The fact that more examples don't come from the less able groups I teach is of regret to me and is I admit because there are fewer examples on which to draw to demonstrate my argument. I believe the reasons for this to be concerned with my own inadequacies as a teacher; with my ineptness at setting up situations where enthusiasm can flourish rather than any inability on the part of the children to experience enjoyment of the subject.

I hate teaching statistics, I enjoy teaching algebra; guess whose class hates statistics and whose class does well in algebra! I admit to talking a great deal to my groups, so I know that a study of my classroom would reveal an inordinate amount of monologue. When introducing a topic in statistics, I begin to lose the class after only a few minutes and it is time to get them working on a related problem. On the other hand I have often been amazed to hear the bell go and I'm still rambling on about factorizing quadratics and the group is still listening! Poor practice on my part, but the point I am making is: why did they listen to me for an hour with no respite when on another day they can hardly manage five minutes?

I recently conducted an anonymous survey among my third year group – a 'banda' of the 'What do you think of the course so far?' variety. 'Please be honest and I won't look while John collects them in'. Nobody admitted to disliking maths ('anonymous they may be, but I bet he can tell!'). However, it was gratifying to see the frequency with which 'I like maths because the teacher makes it interesting' occurred. Unless I am experimenting or taping for some talk or project I freely admit that I teach formally and traditionally subject matter that is also largely traditional, yet they like my lessons, they enjoy working, they have made my enthusiasm their own (well, a lot of them have).

Of course, I am not novel in this respect – any proficient teacher succeeds in a similar manner, but it is not frequently acknowledged that the reason lies in the communication of enthusiasm. My new classes tend to give me some rather old-fashioned looks when they hear a graph described as exciting or they see that an equation makes my hands go up and down, but such eccentricities eventually appear to go unnoticed as they begin to share my interest.

Recently there has been much written on the importance of group work, inter-pupil communication and cooperation and the minimizing of teacher intervention. More of this later, but I wish to stay with the teacher a while longer in an attempt to redress the balance somewhat. The teacher's role in mathematics lessons is vital, firstly because he or she is, or should be, the instigator of the enthusiasm factor I have outlined. Secondly, mathematics is a sequential discipline, one step building upon another and walking up those steps needs direction. Without going into the forms of knowledge it is difficult to make a case for this. I must be satisfied with arguing that even though, ideally, children should be able to discover all for themselves, in reality life is not long enough. Mathematical methods are by no means rigidly laid down and children should get the opportunity to develop novel approaches, but the blind alleys are numerous for the novice and direction and demonstration are essential so that children can be initiated into the processes though not necessarily the methods.

Two pupils may discuss a problem and given time might develop a solution, they may also spend much time on a totally unsuitable approach or because of one misconception believe that they have a viable method when they have not. If they instead discussed the problem with the teacher much time would be saved and the one misconception quickly sorted out. It could be, and is argued that even the wrong approach is useful, that we learn from mistakes, that the positive aspects of two children communicating on a shared problem outweighs any mistakes made. All this is valid, except in terms of practicality and efficiency. Indeed it is hard to assess what is lost by teacher intervention and easier to see what is gained in terms of more problems done in a given time and less time wasted on the wrong tracks. It is a matter of degree – shared problem solving is essential, but so is judicious teacher intervention.

A third vitally important role of the teacher's talk in the classroom is as a demonstration and example of the use of language in a specialized form. The tight formal language of mathematics does not become essential until way beyond school level and yet textbooks and many teachers use it pedantically, e.g. 'line segment' instead of just 'line'. Everyday language can cope very well with mathematics up to the fifth year and beyond without compromising accuracy of expression. The teacher should exemplify this by using plain and varied language only using technical terms after they have been explained and only when it can be shown that to use them is simpler and more efficient.

Mathematical expressions and symbols make up the neatest and most precise of languages and yet at school level they can only be understood by translating them into our spoken language. The teacher can foster understanding by careful use of his or her spoken work, e.g. $3x$ is usually spoken as 'three ex' or even 'three of ex', neither of which makes a whole lot of sense, whereas 'three exes' dispels any mystique and is as obviously correct and clear as saying 'three apples', instead of 'three apple' or 'three of apple'!

Language can be accurate without including a technical vocabulary and the teacher again should seek to demonstrate this: 'The line that joins A and B,' rather than, 'You see that line that goes from there to there.' By repeating, paraphrasing, paraphrasing and repeating, the teacher can help the children make mathematical language their own.

The first step in solving any mathematical task is to translate it into everyday language. We've all had the experience of the child who can't proceed and we say: '. . . read it out to me . . . now what is it about?' and the child goes away happy. The teacher has facilitated the child's own problem-solving by making him or her verbalize it. Talking around problems, looking at them from different angles and asking questions are all strategies for solving problems and indeed for learning at all. Probably it does not matter whether the problem is talked about out loud or silently to oneself, it is the verbalizing that appears to trigger the thought processes; perhaps verbalizing slows down and orders the thoughts so that the information can be analysed step by step. Even intuition, which is so important in maths, can be apparently aided in this way though perhaps it is lightning fast thought anyway. Teachers should develop this thinking aloud process and this is one of the main reasons that talk is so important in the maths lesson. Children should imitate their teachers so that they develop the ability to analyse their own thinking processes.

A fourth role played by teacher talk in the maths classroom relates to modes of inquiry and the asking of questions. We need to review our reasons for asking questions of children. I certainly ask questions for all sorts of reasons and many of them have little to do with strategies for problem-solving. For example, it shook me to realize that one of the most frequent is as a punishment: 'What did I just say, John?' or 'Seeing as you aren't listening you must already know the answer to this. . . .' No wonder I also find myself saying that I wish there were more hands up or that I want to see some of the others answering for a change. Quite unintentionally, I'm discouraging them from answering. Another reason for asking questions is to provide an opportunity for positive reinforcement. 'That's right, well done!' But it's often at the expense of the child who didn't know the answer. All this is very bad practice, and it has taken me years to realize what I am doing. Surely the only valid reason is asking a question as an invitation to discussion and this can only work when it is apparent that I don't necessarily know the answer myself or at least when there is more than one possible answer.

I value teacher-directed class discussion and it does not worry me that only a few may make verbal contributions in any one lesson as long as the rest are attentive. The silent majority still benefit from listening to the discussion. Don't we all attend meetings, lectures and discussions and enjoy the benefits without necessarily participating; our thoughts are still stimulated. It is my task to ensure that everyone has their day for active participation and that no-one feels left out. There is no place for casual chatter especially because of the nature of the subject: solving any problem requires a sequential train of thought, it demands hard application. You can't start an investigation, break for a chat and then return to take it up where you last left it. The chain is broken, you have to go back and start again; no progress can be made like this.

In equal measure I also value group discussion, but here the dangers and pitfalls are greater. I am concerned with teaching mathematics and associated communication skills; socialization skills are of a much lower priority in the maths lesson. In group work inconsequential talk is inevitable and yet cooperation between pupils when working is so vital as a means of finding the way through a problem, as an aid to verbalization and as an incentive to keep at it. Helping each other, discussing it at your own level, and making your own thoughts more clear by endeavouring to explain to your peers are all essential to enjoying and developing the subject. Lack of teacher direction (he or she can't spend so much time with each group if there are many of them), allowing the group to flounder and losing the thread by being sidetracked by casual conversation are the disadvantages. I, personally, compromise by restricting the size of each group – never more than three, but usually only two. This seems to generate a working environment that, as long as the teacher keeps a light finger on the pulse, does not degenerate into noisy chaos. Another comment arising from my anonymous survey was, 'I like maths because you can work with your partner and help each other out.'

Talk between pupils can often help them when talk with the teacher cannot. The teacher inevitably gets a blinkered view of what is going on in front of him or her and may miss the chatter. More importantly his or her interpretation of the child's degree of understanding is often wrong or at best distorted.

John and Peter were working on the problem of how area can change amongst shapes with the same perimeter:

1. *John*: How do you find perimeter?
2. *Peter*: You count the numbers around.
3. *John*: Are you sure?
4. *Peter*: I'll explain in a second. (*He's busy adding up numbers*).
5. *John*: That's not how you do the circle.
6. *Peter*: Oh, the perimeter on the circle is that $2 \pi r$ thing innit?
7. *John*: Perimeter is the circumference sort of, is it?
8. *Peter*: Yes! It's the area around.
9. (*Later – teacher has arrived and they have some results?*)
10. *Teacher*: That's very good. Which shape do you think would have the greatest area for a given perimeter?
11. *Peter*: Er. The decagon I think. . . .
12. *Teacher*: It's the circle.

Peter's explanation (2) of how to find the perimeter is apparently unclear: a teacher would certainly demand clarification and yet John appears to understand without any trouble. It is interesting that John knows more about circumference than perimeter (5-7). A teacher would certainly not choose a circle to explain perimeter, yet it apparently helps John, perhaps because he 'did' the circle quite recently. Peter, who appears to know exactly what's what, commits a serious error in (8) which indicates a certain woolliness in his basic concepts. It is not merely a slip of the tongue that inserts 'area' in place of 'distance', like many children with technique rather than understanding, he can demonstrate the correct answer, fool the unwary teacher that the topic has been grasped and yet have failed to internalize the fundamental concepts involved.

The teacher has to listen, watch, and then to respond with more than everyday sensitivity if he or she is to grasp what the child knows. In lines (10-12), although it is not obvious, the teacher ignores Peter's suggestion. I was so keen to demonstrate that the area increased as the shape approached that of a circle that I missed Peter's comment and only on playing the tape did I realize that he'd even spoken – yet he was on exactly the right lines – he knew the decagon would have the biggest area yet it would have been but a small step to have completed the deduction. I deprived him of that satisfaction because I did not listen carefully. How often do we dampen enthusiasm by only hearing what we expect and by not listening because we have a queue at the desk or a forest of hands in the air?

There are two broad and general philosophies of mathematics which can be used to justify its teaching in schools.

The first is that mathematics exercises and develops an ability and tendency that is part of our human nature; it is a form of knowledge and all knowledge is of intrinsic worth; it carries within itself the seeds of satisfaction; it is a worthwhile thing to do for itself. The process of 'doing' maths successfully is innately satisfying and is therefore a suitable activity for including in the curriculum.

The second philosophy emphasizes the instrumental value of mathematics; what it can do. It argues that the true worth lies in its applicative nature; maths is useful, a necessary tool for life. We need to be able to check our change, calculate how much carpet we want and to budget our wages. On a less mundane level, mathematics is a construct of our minds, it is abstract, but can impose order on our interpretation of the world; its essential value is extrinsic.

Current views of mathematics teaching favour the second of these outlooks. Cockcroft et al. want solid, empirically verifiable and assessable aims. They see maths as a tool on which children need to get a firm grip if they are to fit into our technological society. If they can enjoy fumbling for a hold then this is a bonus, but the main thing is the raising of measurable performance. Shades of 'back to basics'? No, that would be hotly denied!

I would suggest that such an emphasis tends to lead to a preoccupation with training rather than educating, but I will not pursue that argument here. For our present purposes, I would like to indicate a further danger of the second type of philosophy.

Let us consider motivation in the learner. The child will not learn efficiently without some internal driving force, so what makes a pupil want to learn mathematics? The answer is all too frequently, 'Not a lot'.

'It will help me get a job,' is a frequent response when a child is asked why he or she wants to do maths, but such a reason can only really motivate a tiny percentage of first, second or third years. Such a reason is too remote for the majority to seriously take it into account when faced with the decision between doing the maths homework and going out with your mates, or between listening to the teacher and throwing inky darts at Robert.

We also know that extrinsic compulsions to work and learn such as those that might arise from a strict authoritarian regime fail to provide healthy motivation and rote learning plus skill acquisition rather than understanding seem to be general characteristics of such environments. Of course we all know the answer to the motivation question, don't we? Make it interesting! How often have we heard that cry and how true it is. If you can interest children there is no end to the endeavour they will undertake and you have a situation where real learning and understanding can develop.

Children need to enjoy learning and too many do not enjoy learning mathematics. Emphasizing the applicative worth of mathematics however can lead imperceptibly to a false conclusion; namely that children will be interested by (and will therefore enjoy) mathematics that is useful and relevant and practical.

Whole courses have been built on this mistake. How can we motivate these children to learn mathematics? Answer: we will build a syllabus out of everyday arithmetic problems. It will be the sort of thing they will need when they leave school and because it is relevant to their life outside school (they all look at their gas meters and measure up for carpets at home, don't they?), they will find it interesting and will want to do it. Now stand back and watch the course founder because they don't want to do it. Relevance and practicability do not automatically lead to wanting to do something. Knowing that you should does not mean the same as knowing that you want to.

Of course, the useful side of mathematics needs to be presented and of course, its application to everyday problems should be exercised, but when looking for enjoyment and wanting to do it. When motivating children, then look to the first philosophy.

The problem is, of course, how to give a child the opportunity to experience the satisfaction obtainable from manipulating the pure principles and processes of mathematics. It is apparent that it is denied the majority and it is claimed that to do maths at the level required to experience this intrinsic enjoyment is beyond all but the gifted mathematicians. This I deny; all children can become interested in the patterns and rules for their own sake. Recently in a remedial group I observed the delight a lad experienced in discovering that there were as many odd as even numbers in the series 1-100.

Small beginnings, but even at this stage he had enriched his total experience: (1) it was satisfying to have found out something that was not known before and satisfaction is addictive; (2) the pattern was striking – it was the same number. Now in the future he might look in similar situations for patterns of this sort and if he only asks, 'Are the two numbers the same?' that future experience will have acquired a dimension it might not have had. At one level the example demonstrates learning from empirical observation, but the point is that it had no specific application, no particular use and yet it was valued by the child for itself or for himself.

Much of what I have said may appear reactionary and my emphasis on teacher talk will certainly be met with many objections and criticisms. I readily admit to shortcomings in my teaching methods, but adhere strongly to my key argument: the teacher being a source of enthusiasm is the prerequisite for successful mathematics education in our schools. Maths teaching has had a dire history in this country; it is a well worn cliche to say, 'Oh! I hated maths when I was at school,' and it is time that it was put to rest.

The enthusiasm once sown must be nurtured by teachers who are prepared to think carefully about the talk they promote in their classes and about the words they use and about how talking about maths can assist understanding. We must create a secure and sympathetic environment so that this can all take place; so that questions can be freely asked on both sides and so that children can develop the confidence to talk about maths while teachers listen.

Chapter 7

Language and learning in English

Elaine Mount

In this chapter, Elaine Mount describes the way in which English is taught in the school and attempts to define what is distinctive about language and learning in English. She discusses the responsibility of the English teacher to provide a context in which students can develop their use of language, secure in the knowledge that what they say will be valued.

Obviously we see our job as most others do, to encourage students to look upon themselves as individuals and as being in a position to control language both with respect to their talking and their writing. Our main objective is that by providing a suitable environment and providing a balance of learning experiences they will become skilled users of language.

In some ways it's not easy to recognize the learning that's going on in English because it is not a knowledge-based subject tied to facts and information but we have got a content, a very important one, and our aim is that through talking, writing and reading, we hope to introduce students to it.

If we think about the content of English, the ideas, facts, references to the world and so on that we broach, the most striking thing about it all is that a large proportion of it has come into our classrooms with the students rather than been presented by us. This, we see as a distinction between our subject and those where predominantly the content comes from the teacher either directly or through books and other teaching aids and the teacher selects material and structures it according to what he or she wants the students to learn. In English, though we may introduce a topic or some material, our main concern is to relate it back to what the students already know. Our emphasis is to get them to deal with the material in a way that suits them, according to the material that's already in their heads. Because of this the content and the learning is of course often unpredictable but having the students deal with the material in their terms, bringing in their past experiences, is to give them the opportunity to understand the school experience more fully. The knowledge they have already is used to push them on to new knowledge and awareness, new ideas and a greater control over language.

If the students coming into the school are encouraged to use their language and they realize it's valued, then their confidence grows, they develop self-awareness, change their view of themselves and feel they've got something valuable to contribute. If that happens then we're on the way to success because then they're not just receivers of our language in the classroom but they become confident language users and realize what they want to use language for.

As students begin to know what they want to use language for, it becomes our job to encourage them to become independent learners, giving them control of what they do and ultimately what they learn from it. Here we try to make sure that when we give a suggestion for doing something we also stress that investigating other ways of doing it is just as valuable. We take ourselves away from being just givers of tasks and speakers of monologues.

Talking and listening

Talk is, of course, of central importance to all subjects and small-group talk is an intrinsic part of English bound up in the network of activities of talking, writing, reading and listening.

The way we organize small-group talk is, as far as possible, through self-chosen groups. This is because the confidence of all the kids is obviously much greater than when they have to work with people that they don't really know. The English teacher's crucial part then is to provide the social context where the kids are able and willing to use language effectively. We try to make sure that the atmosphere is light because no-one can use language to the best of their ability unless they're in a situation where they're comfortable and relaxed. Apart from having a pleasant talk area and a suitable arrangement of furniture, it also means that accents, dialects (and, of course, other languages) are valued and given a place. The sort of atmosphere where kids can make their language explorations and their speculations without fear of ridicule or contradiction would ideally happen in a full class talk situation too, but this happens infrequently because of personality differences and rivalries so that the necessary atmosphere is more often than not just too difficult to achieve.

We're probably all guilty of making assumptions about what we think students know and in English, through small-group talk, we've found that many skills exist and are used that we didn't know about.

We've found that when students talk in groups without adults present they learn a great deal. Responsibility for management falls upon them. They must decide who talks and when, they have to cope with conflict and silences. They have to encourage each other, control dominant people and decide what's worthwhile. Whilst all this is going on they're using their own language. They have the opportunity to explore new topics in their terms and their language, using the knowledge they already have to reshape any materials we give them.

The more a teacher intervenes in this sort of set-up the more the students feel they have to keep to a pattern. Teachers often fear that in small-group talk the students will get distracted. I would like to suggest that the teacher may need to provide explicit objectives for any students who aren't used to working in this way but that in general the students can, and should, be trusted.

Another point worth mentioning about small-group talk is that it helps in the development of listening skills. Small groups are far better training grounds for listening than larger groups. We all know the problems we experience in trying to get the attention of a whole class or getting a whole class to listen to a fellow student. If students are talking in smaller groups, they are able to understand the language and, in my experience, always give space for everyone to talk and listen.

A couple of final points worth mentioning about small-group talk and learning in English are that block timetabling allows much more time for talk to develop and extend. Lower school English has whole morning or afternoon sessions where talk can develop, and tape recordings be used. When tape recorders are used and talk monitored, points can be taken up later about sidetracking, difficulties and so on. It's not necessary to go into the value of the use of tape recorders here but they have considerable value for assessment purposes and when talk is to lead to writing. Students love listening to themselves too. A tape recorder can be a great incentive to talk!

Teacher talk is also crucial to learning in the classroom. Even though English teachers do not have to convey many 'facts', we do present material and function as a point of reference for the students. The social relationship between pupils and teacher affects talk and learning and the more comfortable the environment, both physical and psychological, the more effective is the teaching likely to be.

We place importance on using chat, anecdote and jokes with both the teacher and students taking part and sharing experience. We feel that if the teacher goes in as the dominant talker, that establishes a pattern of talk and gives the students a passive role. We always strive to make sure that we're sensitive to what the students say, as the wrong response from the teacher can close down the students' language explorations. When we have reflected on our whole-class discussions, we have found we are often guilty of accepting too quickly some of the comments offered and this had the same effect as above, blocking any deeper explorations.

Writing

As opposed to learning through talk, learning to write is much more difficult for many students: some get a great deal of personal pleasure out of it while others achieve only minimal competence. We hope in English to try and help all students to enjoy writing; to help them see themselves as writers and to see writing as a purposeful activity. There are two important things which contribute to this. Firstly, students attempting to write should be aware of an audience and we feel that they should know their writing is going to be seriously received by the reader. Secondly, each writing task should allow the writer to discover more about what he or she thinks and feels. If we want to fulfil our aims then, writing must suggest a real purpose to students, not just be a practice, a mechanical duty to satisfy school demands. Unless the meaning and significance are present there'll be no satisfaction and enjoyment and consequently no real learning.

Aside from literature and some project work, English lessons are essentially for hearing about things that happen outside school, in the home, with friends or in their imaginations and, although I've just talked about the crucial significance of talk in English, students need to write about their experiences as well and share them with others that way.

The obvious place to start is with the students' own experiences, with the resources which they bring into school with them in their heads and which they have the ready-made language for. The task here can be teacher or student initiated and immediately reinforces that what they have to offer is valuable. From then on the writing can develop into story writing, poetry and so on. As I said earlier, we provide starting points but tend to stress that these are possibilities rather than prescriptions. Not allowing for variation can lead to stilted writing but on the other hand, complete freedom of choice leaves a lot of students struggling, especially those who are struggling with the writing system itself. Freedom of choice only fully reaches those who want to write. The rest complain they've got nothing to write about, which usually isn't true but is a display of a lack of confidence in their ability which we have to overcome.

The structure of writing and its creativity are essential to each other and we recognize both. They can perhaps best be explained in terms of the craft and art of writing (McLeod and Richmond, 1981). The craft of writing is obviously more visible than the art. This in itself can be a problem because many of us concentrate too readily on what we see. The craft of writing concentrates on errors and confusions in writing, style and grammatical complexity. For the students the craft of writing is made visible in activities such as:

- pre-writing (what the students do before the pen hits paper),
- looking back over work and revising,
- proof-reading after writing,
- discussing with friends or the teacher,
- redrafting as desired.

However, we are also I think, achieving some success by treating as priorities pleasure in writing and emphasizing the overall shaping process.

This emphasis on the art of writing leads to a focus on:

- the topic of the writing.
- sense of involvement, purpose and direction,
- sense of audience,
- writing as means of self-expression and coming to terms with oneself.

Taking this approach concentrates attention on:

- the writer's confidence,
- the students' view of writing and themselves as writers,
- motivation to write,
- originality and individuality.

We don't set the craft and the art in a hierarchy; both are important to each other and bound up together. Nor do we deal with the two separately. The sorts of help we offer the craft are, for example working on one aspect of their errors at a time or emphasizing that they should look for their own mistakes through writing and reading their work, drafting and redrafting. As far as is possible we see students on a one-to-one basis, talking about errors rather than just marking them and we encourage students to help each other by commenting constructively on each other's work. At all times, we try to keep their sights on the overall purposes they have in writing and the effects they hope to have on their readers.

Reading

Our aims in dealing with literature are to avoid personal responses being destroyed. Kids should both get enjoyment and be enabled to make meaningful interpretations of what they read but there are problems involved in enabling students to combine the simple pleasure of reading fiction with a more critical approach. They need to be guided as they get older to a variety of forms of writing, some of which may be less directly relevant to their immediate lives and where they may have to struggle over the words on the page.

We approach literature through individual reading, students bringing books in, using class libraries and the school and public libraries. We talk with them about the books they are reading. We also approach literature through group reading, small groups or whole class. This is important because then the students can relate their own responses to the responses of others. This sort of shared experience is valuable. With less accessible material the work can then easily be talked about and individuals don't need to worry that they're the only ones not to understand. As they gain independence in reading we encourage wider personal reading, talking with them and giving them guidance. We want to reflect, talk, write and read more (e.g. by same author). Through this sort of exploration on a text a deeper insight will be gained.

As, with talk and writing it seems important to give the students a sense of responsibility for their own learning. This means allowing students to:

- Take up a viewpoint from different characters, thus understanding the viewpoints of several people and their characterization – role plays and writing.
- Work on converting a story to a radio play. This gets students involved in text and makes them responsible for the outcome. They have to interpret and be creative, use dialogue from the story and make up dialogue to cover descriptive parts of the story. The emotion behind characters' words has to be understood and they have to probe and pose questions to themselves.
- Rewrite parts of stories in another context gets students to pose questions, rethink, search through their language to express themselves appropriately. They come to terms with the perhaps, at times, alien language of the text through their understanding of the alternative context.

Chapter 8

In the English classroom
Dave Lewis and Elaine Mount

In this chapter, Dave Lewis and Elaine Mount describe in detail a sequence of work undertaken in a first-year English class. They consider a small group of boys of differing backgrounds and abilities as they set about a succession of tasks, including the making of a radio programme. By analysis of recordings made in the classroom, they show that not only do the shyer and less spontaneously vocal students gain confidence but that they also develop new roles and skills and become able to take an active role in shaping the group's concerns, during these activities.

Over a ten-week period, we tried to monitor the progress of a single, small group of pupils through a succession of different tasks, all of which involved, in varying degrees, the use of collaborative talk. We wanted to examine, in particular, the relationship between the constraints each task imposed and the different effects these constraints had on the group, and also, the patterns of relationship which emerged between group members.

We had expected that the group (of first-year pupils), being newly formed would initially be tentative together, and that, given the composition of the group, two of them would be likely to play a dominant role – setting the pattern of the talk and controlling the strategies used in tackling the tasks. However, we also expected (or perhaps, hoped) that there would be a gradual 'balancing out' as the tasks and weeks went by; the shyer, more withdrawn would become more confident and begin to assert themselves, to contribute more, while the more forceful would adjust accordingly to a lower key as they accommodated the others. We thought that eventually, towards the end of this series of lessons, a strong and successful bonding and rapport might develop between the members of the group, and that this would be reflected in an increasingly effective management of their work together.

The group that we focused our attention on consisted of four boys

(Steven, Mahesh, Riaz, Graeme), in a first-year mixed-ability English class. We wanted the tasks, the lessons, and the contexts to be as typical as possible. As one of us, Elaine, was the class's regular English teacher, and as they were already familiar with collaborative talk situations, these conditions could be, to some extent, easily met.

We decided that all the tasks would involve predominantly oral activity, and that the actual work done by the different groups would be largely 'independent', with the teacher being minimally present as a guide if needed.

The task which was deemed by all concerned to be the most successful, the one in which there was the most engagement, was that of the making of a radio magazine. The class had been coming to the end of some project work based on a school siege: pupils with a dangerous virus trapped for weeks inside their school. The project was to be completed by the class working in small groups as teams of programme producers who were to feature the ending of this siege on their radio programme. They could organize the feature as they liked – interviews with pupils and with distressed parents, were two of the suggestions made in a preliminary class discussion. The class was told that the rest of the programme could be filled up with anything they thought suitable. Again, several suggestions were made as to the kinds of items such radio programmes might contain.

There were several aspects of the task itself which we considered contributed to its success.

Firstly, there was the degree of open-endedness. The format was, in a sense, partly open-ended, partly directed. There was a clearly defined end product – a complete programme, which had to contain, as a main feature, the ending of the school siege – but there were no other directions given as to the make-up of that end product. Thus there was considerable scope for free improvization within the constraints which the radio magazine structure would impose. In the group's finished product there were these following items: a section on the school siege consisting of interviews with the relevant people involved; a solo singing spot; a news report on an oil strike; an interview with a football star's wife; football results, and several recipes, all delivered with a variety of accents and accompanied by, and interspersed with, a variety of sound effects.

Not only did this 'openness' allow for such a range of contexts for talk, but it also encouraged participation from all members of the group. As one, Steven, perceptively pointed out afterwards: '. . . each has a part to contribute – different accents, playing different parts . . . plenty of variety.' They could all participate in the areas in which they felt most confident. Thus Steven sang, Graeme made up silly recipes, Riaz displayed his American accent, and Mahesh (with assistance) made up football results. Graeme, another member of the group, made the point afterwards, 'we could do what we liked on it, we didn't have to do something specific. . . .'

The combined openness and collectivity of this task undoubtedly contributed to its success. And, no doubt, there were other significant factors. But to explain the reasons for the success of this task, or indeed of any others, simply in terms of the qualities of the task itself, divorced from its context, would be a mistake. What is more important is the pupils' perspective of the task. How do they individually and/or as a group interpret it? To ignore their viewpoint would be to assume that there was a perfect correlation between the teachers' expectations and the pupils' perceptions.

In setting a particular assignment, the teacher has certain aims and objectives. He or she has, no doubt, a particular framework in mind which she expects the pupils to adopt. But the model(s) the pupils are working with may be in important ways different from that of the teacher – and this may be for a variety of reasons which have ramifications far beyond that specific lesson. What kind of relationship do the pupils have with that teacher? What (referring now to our own study) is their experience of, and attitude towards, English or towards small-group work which is predominantly oral? What indications are there that the teacher values their talk and so on? (And there are, of course, wider questions which go beyond those particular classroom relations.) All such factors will influence, to varying degrees, the way the pupils take on each task.

Making a radio programme: Radio Ad Lib

The preliminary class discussion which began the lesson set up the conceptual framework and presented the model which Elaine Mount wished the class to adopt. She began by talking about the newspapers the groups had earlier made on the school siege, about other ways of showing the news and about the idea of the radio magazine. As was mentioned earlier, the programme had to include the ending of the school siege. They could decide on the rest. After a short discussion on the kinds of items the programme might contain and on the recognizable features of radio programmes (jingles, etc.), the groups began their planning. Elaine Mount suggested to them that this planning would best be done on paper first of all.

We had expected the groups to go about the task in a careful, organized way, imitating the typical radio conventions; to formulate a magazine-style programme with some distinct character and flavour to it, blending in roughly equal proportions, the humorous and the sensational.

The group we studied tackled the task in an idiosyncratic way.

They circumvented the advice for planned organization by calling their radio station 'Ad Lib', and thus, in Graeme's words, 'We can say what we want . . . and don't have to put it all down on paper.' This attitude was clearly shaped by the group's previous experience of their drama lessons, in which they plan very briefly and rely mainly on improvisation. For them, much of the enjoyment of drama appeared to lie in improvising in front of an audience. For example, in one drama session, they had been given the task of linking six pictures in a story to be performed for the rest of the class. With performance very much in mind, they treated the planning and putting together of the story scantily – they knew they would improvise in performance, so it did not really matter.

The very name 'Ad Lib' suggests the style, though not the content of the programme. It is obvious that they were keen to get the feature on the ending of the school siege over with quickly and not to take it, as it was intended to be taken, as *the* central item. The point of the programme was not seen, by them, as a vehicle for presenting the final chapter of the school saga; this imposed structure did not really give them the same kind of scope which the rest of the programme would allow, and it is the opportunities of the latter which were uppermost in their minds.

The necessary inclusion of this item created individual differences within the group about what the requirements of a radio programme are:

Steven: Who's going to be the disc jockey?
Graeme: We don't need a disc jockey.
Riaz: We do need a disc jockey, this is radio.

For Riaz, the presence of a disc jockey was seen as a necessary element in any radio programme, and he had not taken on the notion of the magazine format. Graeme, on the other hand, had: he realized that the inclusion of this 'hard news' item meant that the programme would be of a more varied kind than the familiar Capital Radio pop music sort. Instead of a disc jockey, there would be a presenter, a reporter, and so on. He forcefully framed this part of the programme, revealing his definite view as to how they should interpret it:

Graeme: He (*Steven*) can be the presenter and he's going to interview you (*Mahesh*). And you're gonna be the one who . . . who finds it all out and you can come on and say what you find out and I can argue with you. . . .

With this framework, the programme began: the improvization, though still present, taking second place to the conventions inherent in the format. Thus Steven played the inquisitive interviewer, Graeme, the evasive spokesperson for the school, Mahesh, the investigative reporter, and Riaz, a distressed parent.

However, as soon as they became involved in the conversation, they seemed to forget the direction which they ought to have been moving – towards some sort of finale. No doubt the fact that there had been virtually no planning contributed towards this, but that in itself is a reflection of their fundamentally different interpretations of the task. It seems, again, that such considerations weren't taken into account. Instead, they diverted their attention to the fun they could eke out of the situation – mainly, it seems, through Riaz's impersonation of one of the disease victims' mothers:

> *Steven*:   . . . And um here is his parent, who's very very upset about his state. Um, are you fit to talk at the moment?
> *Riaz*:   (*sobbing*) er, yes . . . my boy, my boy, . . . is he alright? Is he alright?
> *Steven*:   Yes, he's okay.
> (*Noises, crying, muffled laughter*).

In this way, the serious context could be deflated. The sense of fun in which all four appeared to perceive the task as a whole, was facilitated by the improvisatory nature of their programme: spontaneous humour and well-worn jokes abounded as topics were exploited for their joke potential.

Clearly, then, at one level, the task was construed by the group as an opportunity for fun. When I asked each afterwards why they enjoyed this lesson, Mahesh said it was because 'it was really funny,' Riaz, that 'there was a lot of jokes in it,' and Steven said it was because 'it was just a bit of fun really'. Indeed, they found the idea of the programme so compelling that they saw no good reason to organize it in the 'professional' way we had expected. The possibility of smooth linking and continuity was further removed by the arrangement of the rest of the programme. Again, because there was no coherent planning, decisions on content seemed to be made mainly by experiment – an item was improvised and if deemed successful it stayed in, otherwise it was rubbed off.

It was clear from the first session we observed that Steven was the dominant member of the group and that initial impression was borne out through the following sessions. At first, it was illustrated by his taking charge of the tape recorder, and later, even more overtly, by the physical arrangement of the group around their set of desks. (The original two-facing-two situation was replaced in the final four lessons by a one-to-three form.) But it was more subtly evident in the tactics and strategies he adopted in the group work through each lesson. The consequences of such leadership were, I think, highly significant. . . . First of all, he could be seen as an initiator – starting off the conversation, making a characteristic framing move to set things in motion; for example:

'Right . . . now we're gonna start the recording.'
'C'mon, let's start.'
'Right, then, shall we get started?'

Now in most of these tasks there was an initial planning stage which preceded the 'performance'. So someone in the group had to start the planning stage (as in the examples above) and then someone had to suggest when to begin the second phase. Again it was Steven who made this, sometimes delicate, move far more than any of the others – using, not unnaturally, the same form of words:

'Right let's start'
'Right, shall we start?'
'Right, then, ready?'

Sometimes this gatekeeping role was used to put a clamp on the wayward progress the group were making. Thus, in making the radio programme, he stepped into the collective singing of the signature tune:

'So right, let's go through it, yeh?'

These responsibilities of initiating, controlling and pacing extended in two directions: firstly, towards a more authoritarian exercising of control over the group, and secondly, at another level, towards a more organizational shaping role. So on occasion, he interrupted both individuals:

'Stop mucking about, Mahesh!'
'Graeme . . . you just said somethin' stupid. . . .'

and the group in general:

'Come on, we're supposed to be doing work. Act sensible.'
'Shut up, shut up. Right, right. Ready?'

And, more importantly, he organized and presented the form of most of the tasks, providing many of the ideas and setting in motion various trains of thought. For example, in the radio magazine task, each little topic – name of radio station, its wavelength, the signature tune – was set in motion by him:

'It's called Ad lib . . . shall we decide on a wavelength? . . .
(*singing*) Capital Radio. . . .'

In another task, compiling a questionnaire, he presented the idea for the topic, which is afterwards taken up by Graeme:

'. . . an overall general knowledge questionnaire – would you believe that – different things. . . .'

In one task – making up a 'fable' – it was his story which was told, in another – making a TV script – it was his idea which was eventually taken up, and his outline of the plot formed the basis of their scripts:

'It's about a family that are just about to survive a nuclear war and how they survive it. It's about er how they be reduced to, you know, scavenging with rats to get food. . . .'

Given this dominant role he played in nearly all the lessons, it is important that he not only put forward sufficient ideas to keep the group's discussion going, but that he also allowed scope for others to put forward their suggestions, to draw out their comments, to include their voices; and to give the impression that the decision-making is open to all. These are all essential requirements for successful group discussion, and are all very skilfully demonstrated by Steven.

Connecting with this apparent openness is the tentative, speculative style in which he couched his own comments and ideas. In one task, when they are trying to work out what the pictures they've been given mean, he presented his views in terms of possibilities rather than certainties, (in contrast to Graeme):

'If you look at it, it looks like there's a window . . . that's probably a road . . . it looks like it's been caught . . . it's probably cast-iron. . .', etc.

When presenting his idea for the TV script, he was consciously defensive and tentative:

'I've got an idea, but it's absolutely – er – nobody would like it.'

When Mahesh was asked afterwards why he thought Steven was a good talker, he replied, 'Because he knows what to say.' This suggests, perhaps, not only that he is full of ideas, or that he's good at expressing himself, but also that his controlling strategies work – his initiating, pacing, intervening, his guidance of the group through the task are successful. They can rely on him and feel secure with him in control. His ability in the metacommunicative side of the discourse is particularly striking. By continually taking charge of this channel, of course, he reasserts his chairperson role, shaping and directing the group planning, or whatever.

When then small group sessions began, it was obvious that both Steven and Graeme were accomplished and confident talkers, and both were willing to take control of the direction the group would take through the task. This can be seen clearly in the first three of these lessons, where Graeme and Steven tend to dominate the proceedings. Mahesh and Riaz inevitably needed to make adjustments in their conversational skills and strategies in order to accommodate themselves in the group with this other pair. However, as the weeks of this working together went by, what was striking is not simply that they gain in confidence – that is surely to be expected given the generally secure atmosphere built up in the group – but that they began to take on and develop new roles and new skills. This is particularly significant in Mahesh's case, for he was the shyer, less spontaneously vocal of the two.

We began to see hints of this development in the fourth session – the task in which they had to make up a 'fable'. Both were active in suggesting ideas for and attentive to the narration of the story. At one point, Mahesh took on the responsibility of focusing the group: 'What shall we do for chapter 3?' And later on, when Graeme was actively disrupting the narrative flow, Riaz interjected taking on the responsibility of returning the group to the story-line: 'Oh, come on . . . he's all alone in the room, right?'

They also took on the role of peacemakers in the dispute which flares up between Steven and Graeme:

Steven: It was your idea to do my story.
Graeme: It wasn't my idea to carry on this long.
Riaz: Come on, let's carry on.
Mahesh: Come on, carry on.
Steven: What do you expect?
Riaz: Come on, carry on.
Mahesh: Yeh.

and their gentle persuasion has the right effect.

However, the most striking signs of development occurred in the later sessions. Take, for instance, the task in which they had to write a TV script. This is how the planning began:

Riaz: What kinda programme(?) we gonna make?
Steven: We wanna make. . . . (*unclear*)
Riaz: Yeh, but what kind?
Steven: I know. . . .

Riaz took on the directing role, initiated the discussion, and demanded explicitness from Steven! And when there was a diversionary joke, he returned them to the point:

Steven: Cornflakes. No. (*Laughter*)
Riaz: C'mon. What kinda – do we want – horror? Space?

And, soon afterwards, hurried them along:

Riaz: Right, come on then, let's make a decision.

But, more important, he was willing to openly oppose Steven's idea for a programme by proposing and defending his own:

Steven: . . . a family, how they survive a nuclear war.
Riaz: If we want to do, er, space film, right, we can do, I know this sounds a bit daft, you know the space shuttle. . . .

In the task which followed, Riaz once again showed he was prepared to present his point of view and argue it through confidently and forcefully to the rest of the group. And in the next lesson, it was Mahesh's turn to play the directing role, organizing and activating the others, imposing – or at least attempting to impose – some sort of discipline on the rather disordered opening:

Mahesh: Come on then, look, what we gonna do . . . when we get on the TV er programme, what we gonna say? . . .

Being prepared also to reject and suggest:

Mahesh: No, look, we all have our (?) of saying it, right? First, Riaz, then me, then. . . .

It is as if, after feeling the need to rely on Steven in the earlier lessons, they were in these later stages beginning to feel confident and capable enough to shed that dependency and to take on more active and individualized roles in the steering and shaping of the group's concerns.

Chapter 9

In the history classroom

Jon McGill

In this chapter, Jon McGill discusses several of his history lessons: one in which the observed talk seems almost exclusively to be incidental to the task in hand; one where he dramatized the content of the lesson; one where he debated issues with the class; and one where the class as a whole acted out the issues. In reflecting on them he focuses on the possibilities for student conversations and the role of the teacher as both major source and also inhibitor of classroom talk.

Kevin is moaning; the topic for consideration is 'the position of women in Victorian society'.

'Sir, all this stuff is about farmers,' is Kevin's plaintive wail. He is reading page 18 while the rest of us are working on chapter 18. In the far left corner, two pupils are discussing the possibility of taking history materials to their PE lesson; one has an injured leg and the other offers to work with him. I am impressed by his eagerness to continue the history work; I'm soon less impressed when I recall the weather, cold and wet – history in the changing room is marginally preferable to football in the rain.

Two girls are discussing conflicting dates which bear upon the topic.

'Gola trainers went out with Cliff Richard,' is whispered to my right. Michael, in front of me, holds file paper in front of his face and practices crossing his eyes. One pupil wants to know the historical background of a *Punch* cartoon, mentioned in the text. I explain, eager to capitalize on this rare curiosity:

'A magazine, supposedly witty, printed humorous cartoons about political issues of the day.'

'Still around today?'

'Yes.'

'Must be a bit tatty by now.'

I wonder if I was set up.

Mohammed relaxes, considers using his pen, stares at it, decides against use, dismantles it, puts it back together, writes on the desk: 'Kevin sticks his tongue up his nose.'

This comment gives rise to general discussion on nose-picking, Kevin the subject of near-Swiftian essays. This topic brings the entire group to life in the way I had hoped our earlier work would give breath to the position of women. Michael bores easily, resumed drumming practice, eyes now uncrossed.

Chris is describing recent folder work he has done. (A revelation, this, since I'd nearly given up on his doing any at all.) David is labouring under the weight of reading; he expresses his desire to leave at Easter to become what he calls a 'Government artist'. Ever the unwary fool, I ask, in all innocence,

'What's that?'

'Drawing the dole, Sir'.

Several pupils seize upon this as an excuse to berate David.

'You can't live off your family all your life,' one says. This is followed by lengthy commentary along the lines of:

'What are you looking at?'

'You.'

'Oh yeah.'

and so on. Tariq calls Chris 'Idi Amin,' since Chris has called Tariq 'Bloomfield'. Carmelo speculates loudly about Mark hitting Tariq in the mouth. Chris discovers that I am writing all this down.

'He's putting us in a book, guys!'

'Cha!'

'Why?'

'To see who talks the most!'

Tony and Michael are now very curious. Paul tells David to: 'Read the bloody thing.'

Tony suggests that I'm really writing to Tariq's Mum. David reckons I've written four pages on Paul alone. Kevin cracks his knuckles. Mohammed yawns (surely not tired from overwork), looks at me, smiles, pretends to read. Tony asks me to ask Tariq what he (Tariq) said; Tariq says, 'Man United for the Cup.'

Tony is obscene in his reply. Mark is discussing dead people. Chris is talking about shepherds' pie and 'mash'. Everyone is still very curious as to what I'm 'on about'. My writing down their conversational snippets is a highlight of their day. I read back to them what I've written, to their considerable amusement.

These snippets of conversation and cursory observations were recorded over the period of one hour during a fifth-year CSE history lesson. The 'task' set was simple; they were asked to read a short chapter in a text concerning the position of women in Victorian society. The framework for this assignment had been set a week previously during lengthy and free-ranging debate on the topic of the equality of women.

That debate, in which every one of seventeen students spoke at least once, was, aside from my having set the topic, quite spontaneous, very informal and certainly to the point. But, for some reason which I am just now beginning to ponder, I did not see it as a useful addition to any analysis of 'talk' in the history teacher's classroom. I've decided that this is largely due to my preconceptions about the nature and role of talk; in particular, quite unconsciously, I had seen the role of talk as quite different from the role of 'class discussion'.

I still view these two as qualitatively distinct. Talk, though not unproductive, is unstructured, indeed, even out of my control! Discussion, on the other hand, is more formal, i.e. I open, close and direct much of what takes place. And, most important, in common with most teachers, I delude myself into thinking that the discussion is really informal, spontaneous, arising almost unsolicited from the students. At the end of the previous week's debate I had congratulated myself on a near-perfect, progressive lesson. One week later, convinced that the previous discussion had set interests, fired energies, I provided the structure for a very formal, if slightly unusual, reading lesson. Few students read the chapter, they were easily distracted, many talked, either openly or furtively. Their conversations had little, or no, connection with the 'position of women'.

Conclusions? I have none, at the moment. However, in my curiosity about classroom conversations is the germ of curiosity about history teaching and talk in general. Two particular aspects invite attention; one draws the spotlight to the connections between teacher exposition and student responses, the other invites age-group comparisons. My own observations push forward a stark and slightly frightening conclusion; that teacher talk may well be largely irrelevant in the history classroom.

Let me enlarge on this. Most teacher talk has two main components; task assignment and clarification, and, secondly 'lectures', information-dispensing talk. Based upon my own experience (and not yet anyone else's) the second feature appears to have grown less and less useful for most pupils below sixth form levels. A recent lesson to fourth year CSE pupils involved lengthy outlines of the origins of trade unions. Though I specifically wanted an information giving lesson I also wanted to entertain. Though I conveyed the information using dramatic language, role play and gesture, I was nonetheless left feeling that, in summarizing the lesson, students would see it simply as the teacher having talked – and remain unimpressed by the pyrotechnics which tried to disguise the fact. The next lesson with these pupils demonstrated that they retained little except the drama and the display. What I said was of little impact and during my 'exemplary' lesson, they had said little.

However, if talk of this kind from the teacher is indeed not effective as we have taken it to be, what then? Assuming (gross assumption, this) that content is reasonable, subject matter digestible, and all else is satisfactory, how does a history teacher come to grips with what seems the obvious need for a more effective technique of teaching/learning?

My own initial grappling with this has been made easier by acceptance of what has been for a long time an obvious feature of schools – teachers talk too much, students too little. In addition, within the schooling process itself, the ethos of control has imparted a qualitative distinction: teacher talk and that's good; pupils talk and that's bad (unless the talk is authorized by the teacher). Teachers' lack of respect for student talk can be seen as a symbol of the ideology of the schooling process. What is needed to make talk of all kinds relevant and viable is a change in teacher behaviour. For many teachers, myself included, it is nearly impossible to be in a classroom where discussion is taking place and not join in, not comment, not guide or direct. However, to be able to do just that might well be a first step towards greater pupil independence in the learning process and would certainly not be an abdication of the teacher's proper role in facilitating learning.

In one class I have attempted to use talk less focused on the teacher's contributions. The topic was, very generally, aspects of the early industrialization of England. Some worksheet multiple-choice questions had drawn reasonable responses and elicited further queries about factory life. I related a brief anecdote about children losing fingers while cleaning machines. This took us into the realm of compensation and, then, to the area of worker-owner factory relations. Pushing desks to walls, we formed a horseshoe of chairs; I became the 'problem poser'; the problem for them, the workers now, was to bring a recalcitrant and cruel owner into a more enlightened relation to workers.

The guidance I gave was minimal. All they were told was that there were solutions. One volunteer acted out the role of owner and I advised her about ways in which a nineteenth-century owner might respond. The others then presented demands ranging from wage rises to better conditions to compensation for injury.

From the results of this unstructured, and here only sketchily outlined, lesson the following conclusions seemed useful. Firstly, the desire to guide was very strong and, in traditional teacher fashion, I initially interrupted when not needed, when pupils had not run out of ideas. Much of my guidance was too restrictive; I wanted specific conclusions to be drawn and I often made my conclusions pre-eminent. Secondly, the pupils did enter very freely, once 'warmed up' into the spontaneity of the situation and they presented a very credible picture of a group learning on the spot. They took the responses from the 'owner' supplied formally by myself and the girl playing that part and shredded them, picking out weak spots. They also seemed quite content to gradually select a leader or two from amongst themselves, allowing them to pick out bits of advice and information from the group. The increased animation within the group extended to all of the participants: they listened to each other and to me on those, by now fewer, occasions when I interrupted.

By the end of the lesson, my main objective, to open up the possibility of worker organization in the nineteenth century, had been partially met. The pupils had, with little prompting, arrived at their own 'solution', involving unions, meetings, pickets; that conclusion had, I felt, much more significance than those I could have presented wholesale, to them, by 'lecture' or by text. Throughout the lesson I could not quite, however, get free from the tyranny of syllabus or the feeling that our noise spilled into other rooms. And, perhaps most important, while I was certain the lesson had achieved a longer-lasting impression, I was, as yet, still slightly confused about how and where talk could be best used to overcome the drudgery of textbook history.

The teaching of history has often meant a one-dimensional lecture-based or text-based approach and exchanges, teacher to pupil and pupil to pupil, have been underused and undervalued as a means of historical discovery and learning. This is, I think, in part, due to the stranglehold upon the subject still exercised by universities and examination boards. History too often appears to be preconstructed. The part is presented as the story of what happened and little more. When presented with this *fait accompli* there is little to say except repeat 'facts'. Once this approach holds sway, the opportunities which allow children to construct and reconstruct are limited.

Talk makes possible the restructuring of knowledge: a creative history emerges when pupils are enabled to discuss the whys and wherefores and this can then, in theory, be applied as a means of creating the present and future.

Creative talk, talk as a means of discovery has been consigned, in the past, to the catch-all of English classrooms. The rationale is usually that English is less syllabus constrained, less formal as a subject. By implication then, other syllabus areas, already given, dealing with a body of knowledge, are closed to certain uses of language in the classroom. In my view, history teachers need to define for themselves what talk is and what it can do in the classroom. There is a wide range of choices as to how we can measure the success of talk experience. Talk can take many forms: it can be a means toward thoughtful use of evidence; it can have an impact on written products; talk can inform teachers about the nature not only of the tasks set but of pupils themselves. Talk can on the one hand be guided toward the realms of critical analysis or it can, quite simply, be allowed to occur so as to convince pupils that they work in a class atmosphere which is nonrestrictive and flexible. To this end, teachers have to allow for changes in their perceptions of pupils' needs and pupils' views.

Is talk just our latest pacifying ruse? I'm not certain; I have however, been convinced that teachers can sometimes adopt the role of participant rather than leader and that many secondary pupils can and do work out amongst themselves more meaningful historical realities than those we 'teach'. Talk may not revolutionize; it is definitely not new. It is one more method for history teachers whose work may all too often be bound within very narrow confines. Specifically, it may help teach us to rely much more upon school students as they are. They are capable of taking us much further than, in the past, we've wanted to go.

Chapter 10

In the primary classroom

Chrissy Smith

In this chapter, Chrissy Smith explores and extends her thinking about talk in a third-year classroom in one of the feeder primary schools. In response to requests that she provide a point of comparison for the secondary teachers, she made tapes of four different activities in her classroom. She observes that children in some situations are capable of working together with great concentration and animation but, in other contexts, can be subject to considerable anxiety about whether they are meeting the teacher's requirements. Some tasks appeared to increase tension and decrease confidence while others were conducive to confident, logical, and methodical talk. She points to the expectations of the teacher and proposes that opportunities for talk play a key role in the development of student autonomy.

Talk in the primary classroom has always held fascination for me, because, as a primary school teacher, I often feel that I do not give my pupils enough time to talk. The reason is obvious. We tend to undervalue talk, only giving it value when it can be put in a safely bound context, e.g. 'We shall talk about the Christmas play now.' I was worried by our apparent need to keep control of all talk and I wanted to look at those other areas of talk that we, as teachers, tend do this through taping children at work. Teachers like order and encourages, pupil talk. The facets of talk are many but I wanted to find out how many we actually allow into the classroom. I decided to look at four areas of talk that were possible in the classroom and to do this through taping children at work. Teachers like order and methodology and I wanted some kind of structure from which to work. What came from that structure was both surprising and stimulating in terms of the range of language that was uncovered and insights into the ways children make adult language their own.

During the running of the project, I made four tapes only two of which I managed to transcribe (transcription is both laborious and extremely difficult). The tapes were of groups of children in a mixed-ability, multi-ethnic third-year junior classroom and were made while the remainder of the class were at school assembly. This was to avoid background noise and it needs to be said that I regularly kept groups back from assembly to work on various subjects. The children were used to working in small mixed-ability groups for some of the day but maths work was usually done in ability groups. The four tapes I made can loosely be labelled thus:

1. The use of *functional language* in terms of explaining a specific problem to each other and solving it, such as in maths.

2. *Consensus language* in relation to the written word where it was important for the group working together on the task to agree on the eventual written outcome.

3. *Free expression* within the context of an art-based task, where the children were involved in making something, but the talk didn't necessarily have to be about the task in hand.

4. *Democratic discussion*. Here the pupils knew that the task they were set required a certain amount of agreement. How they did this, though, was decided by themselves. A loose structure was given and they were given relative freedom for discussion.

Perhaps I need to add here that I did not always 'use' the same children for my 'experiments'. However, I admit to engineering the shape of the groups because I wanted a mix of talkers and personalities, in order that I didn't get an empty tape where all the shy pupils couldn't bring themselves to speak. On tapes one and three, the children knew they were being taped, and on two and four they were totally unaware until after the completion of the task. This fact is relevant both in terms of how the language of the children changed in relation to the cassette recorder, and also how it changed the tone of the talk that ensued.

When one plays back a tape over and over again, there are always aspects to be discovered that weren't noticed before. This being so, I have only picked out the most important issues that come to light on each tape that are relevant to the kind of talk children indulge in in order to make adult language and tasks relevant to their knowledge and experience. Because I have not transcribed large quantities of tape, the reader will have to accept on trust that my generalizations are based on hours of attentive listening.

Functional language

For Tape One I asked eight children of varying maths ability to work on a specific task – set out on cards – taken from the Derbyshire Maths Programme. Those children who had already grasped the concept inherent in the task helped those who were finding difficulty. Once the children had, more or less, got over the fact that they were being taped, they set about the task. The task set is relatively self-explanatory when one reads the transcript:

A: The digits in the magic square should make the same total when added in any direction. What is the total? Copy one square into your book and fill in the spaces. (*Said in a reading-out-loud style.*)

B: Read it again.

A: (*Reads the card again.*)

C: Tell her how to do them? Y'know.

A: How do you do it? (*Asking if B knows how to do it.*)

B: I dunno. (*Giggles all round.*)

A: What you have to do is erm . . . these are the digits right . . . I think these are the digits.

D: What does digit mean?

B: What does that mean? } (*Simultaneously*)

A: . . . and this is the magic square.

C: Here, I'll tell you what to do listen.

E: Digits mean the numbers. } (*Simultaneously*)

C: I'll tell her what to do. Y'see look . . . look . . . what . . . what's 7 & 6 & 5?

B: 9, 8, 7.

B: Add.

C: Yeah.

D: 19. No . . .

A: 18.

C: 18. Right so . . . what do you need . . . what's 9 & 7?

B: 9, 10, 11, 12 (*Counting on fingers.*)

A: 16.

C: Right . . . how many . . . how many . . . what number should you put up there to make 18?

B: 2.

C: So, put 2 up there . . . . get it? You put all the numbers down . . . you can go ANYWHERE you like and they should add up to 18. (*Lots of mumbling and agreement that they have understood.*)

A: So – say it again – go on.

B: So they should always add up to 18 . . . ?
C: So . . . what's 9 & 6 . . . shh . . . let her do it. (*Meaning B.*)
B: (*Counts it up*) it's 12. (*Giggles all round.*)
C: No it's 15. So how many numbers do you need to make 18?
B: 3.
   (*Giggles*)
B: 5.
C: Sure?
B: Yeah.
C: Sure?
B: No.
   . . . .
C: Right what's 5 & 3?
B: 5, 6, 7, 8!
C: Right – so what number do you need up there to make 18?
B: (*Takes a long time to work it out. Half want to tell her – half want her to work it out on her own*)
   10!
C: Good! . . . all you have to do is keep on putting numbers in . . . not any old number. . . .
B: You have to make 18.

So, what comes out of the tape is the fact that C wants B to understand the task set and is prepared to work at it until she does. C, in actual fact, talks and explains really fast during the whole of the tape, almost as though the faster he talks the better effect he will have on his peer who was trying to grasp the concept. I, as a teacher, have also found myself doing this, but the difference is that C has made the language which I might have used to explain the task his own. It is not intimidatory. There is no antagonism; no 'bullying' technique being used. I know this has something to do with the general friendliness of the class but I also think it has much to do with how the group see the task given. They sense its importance, if only to the teacher, and they in turn are given importance by the nature of the task, and want to complete the task because of the responsibility given them. I didn't deliberately engineer the task to work that way but I did ask those who knew how to do the maths in question to help those who felt a bit unsure. In spite of the fact that I had a complete mix of children working on a mathematical task that they would have normally worked on in ability groups, there seems to be no battling between the cleverest and the poorest, just a willingness to help each other.

I don't mean by this that there is, on the tape, an almost angelic-like quality of cooperation. While Jyotika (B) is having difficulty adding nine and six and Gursharan (C) is doing his best to help her, the rest of the group are giggling at her inabilities, but there is absolutely no hint of malice in their laughter. On listening to the tape frequently, I have come to the conclusion that they are really laughing at Gursharan! He has taken on the teacher role and Jyotika is his pupil. All the children see the funny side of this and the talk progresses with this fact kept in view.

Consensus language

I think, of all the children I recorded, the Tape Two is the most salutary. On this tape, eight children of mixed ability were asked to complete a comprehension test. They had to read the text and then answer the set questions. This tape related to Tape One in that the task set is teacher orientated and is testing certain skills (reading, writing and recording) in an educationally 'set' pattern. Where this tape differs is that the children needed to confer with each other in order to record the end results whereas in Tape One they knew the end result (the right answer) but had to confer at greater length on how to get there.

While on Tape One we have seen that the core of the talk is about a mathematical task, with the need for them to understand and accept something outside themselves to be true, the central language activity on Tape Two is coming to an agreement on how to write down language appropriately. This was the tape from which I discovered most about the children I teach. So many issues emerged that all I feel equipped to do is to transcribe the most relevant parts of the tape, then to list, with brief analysis, my discoveries.

The first part of the tape is taken up with reading out the comprehension piece by all the members of the group of eight, in turn. The piece is about a robin eating a spider, while a toad looks on from the summerhouse. The toad muses on the fact that the spider has met his just fate, as he looks at the spider's web full of the skeletal remains of various insects. . . .

Five minutes are taken up with organizing themselves to write, with me as teacher organizing them as to how to work.

Some time is also taken up with reciting 'Incy Wincy spider', which I thought would help them to relate to the task and put them at their ease.

A short example will illustrate their style of working:

A: '. . . he put his head to one side to show his black eye.'
        Yeah something like that.
B: '. . . to show his black eye'. . . .
A: (*Reads it through again as if confirming her decision to use that particular phrase as the answer.*)

	I'm going to get Ms . . . to show us.
B:	'To show his black eye,' that's what I'm going to put . . . is that what you're gonna put?
A:	Yeah. . . .
B:	I'm just gonna write it. . . .
	(*Interval*)
B:	(*Reading*) 'then he flew inside the summerhouse'.
A:	No. . . .
B:	It *does*! Look, 'then he flew inside the summerhouse'.
C:	Is there a summerhouse!? . . . oh yeah!
A:	Look, it does ask you, 'In to what building did the robin fly?'
B:	I'm gonna write that. . . .
	(*Interval*)
B:	(*In answer to another question.*) I'm just gonna write 'window'.
A:	Well I'm going to write 'perched on the window'.
D:	Window's not right.
E:	It is. ⎱ (*Simultaneously*)
F:	It is. ⎰
B:	It might not be . . .
E & F:	It is.
	. . . .
E:	'What did he do while he was there?'
F:	Gobbled up the spider!
A:	⎱ Yeah.
B:	⎰
A:	That's what I put. . . .
E:	Yeah, look Kisher.
B:	'He gobbled up the spider.'

1. As a group, there is a great deal of listening going on, perhaps because the eventual outcome is a piece of writing. There is definitely a great 'taking in' of other's spoken words.

2. Through this there is a very strong group feeling, as though the group's use of language will help formulate the writing.

3. There is also a searching for reassurance from others in the group. Again, perhaps because a written task is at hand.

4. Oddly enough this search for group consensus doesn't automatically lead to the appointment of a leader. No-one takes leadership, although some voices are louder than others – the group works together as a whole, although it is divided at times.

5. The divisions are strongly sexist. I feel that if a leader had been

appointed it would have been a boy – knowing the class, there is only one girl who would have been likely to take the lead automatically, and I had not included her in the group. At some points in the tape, the girls and boys are working separately from each other. Then at certain intervals they come together. This could be for one or two reasons: either that the girls are better at 'writing down' sentences than the boys, or that there is a genuine coming together once decisions have been made in the separate camps.

6.   All group tasks need an anchorage. On the maths tape it was the cards and the actual drawing of the squares to complete the problem. In this tape there is constant reference to the text throughout. Because I was not always with the group and at one point left the room I was surprised at how well they did stick to the task. This may be something to do with the fact that the task was relatively mechanistic – something which holds its own appeal.

7.   There was no question at all about whether the task was a worthy one. I don't think the children even thought to question it. They just did as they were bid.

Overall, the talk on this tape, although constantly dotted with apparent deviations, adheres so closely to the task that the deviations can immediately be seen either as light relief from the task, or as preparation for the task. Some talk, for example, centres around sharpening pencils, getting rubbers and papers prepared. Hardly any of it could be called 'irrelevant'. I was, perhaps, pleasantly surprised to see that the children wanted to talk about the work set so readily and this talk held many positive qualities not necessarily reflected in the writing.

Free expression

By comparison, on Tape Three the talk the children engaged in is not about the task in hand. The art task was adhered to and the talk could be said to be incidental. Moreover the task here had nothing to do with written or read language as in Tapes One and Two. A skill was being introduced, and the talk that ensued still enabled the skill to be consolidated, even though the talk was not about the skill. The children on the tape are making paper flowers with wire stems – a fiddly and painstaking task – and the tape begins with the usual questions about equipment. Once this has been discussed the children settle down and, because there is an unspoken rule that they are allowed to talk in art, they begin to talk quite freely. An example is not needed to show the content of this talk but it is worth saying that, by listening to this tape, it is clear that by comparison with Tapes One and Two their talk has greater freedom and more confidence. On Tape Two there is evidence of a certain anxiety. They don't really know whether they will be able to complete the task satisfactorily. They are torn between what is satisfactory for them and what is satisfactory, or right, for the teacher. None of these worries appear on Tape Three because the task in hand is visual and active. They are creating something out of materials, they have not been asked to create something out of words. This confident talk also means that the voices become louder. They are not louder because they are seeking attention but because they are confident in what they are saying. Because of this there is no need for group consensus – they are confident within themselves – not because they feel they can make paper flowers well but because they can cope with the task.

The children on this tape are very much on their own. They stand out as individuals secure in their own uniqueness. One child sings quietly to himself as he completes his work. Another two are talking about a film. Another is chattering to anybody, about anything but still doing the task. How is it that we let this talk happen in an art-based task and are less happy that it should happen in a language-based, abstract task? The dividing line is fine. Both kinds of talk are valuable, but it is often only the formal kind that is given explicit credibility by the teacher. I am usually prepared to let 'free' talk go on in an art lesson, but not so in an English comprehension lesson.

Democratic discussion

On Tape Four, I was quite arbitrary in whom I picked for the ensuing 'talk'. They were children with whom I had built up a strong relationship, in and out of the classroom, and the talk was about the forthcoming sports day. I introduced the subject, asking them to take into account that the races to be held were for infants as well as juniors and that they should decide on the races to be held according to age as well as ability. After a short talk on this, I left the room and they got on with it. On listening to Tape Four I was amazed at how well the children kept to the structure I had set for them.

The children knew what they had to do, decided on a logical method to do it and set about the task with great animation – always keeping to the point.

A: Miss, the infants can have easy ones.
T: Like what?
B: They can have a hopping race.
C: Skipping.

B: Jumping.
A: Yeah . . .
    . . . .
B: First let's list all the classes. . . .
    No, let's all say a race, you first, then Kisher, then. . . .
D: Let's have a vote. Who wants that?
B: Yeah . . . who wants the infants to have . . . um . . . skipping
    through the hoops?
E: That would be hard 'cos. . . .
D: Yeah too hard.
C: We could have hopping. . . .
B: Yeah, alright hopping. . . .
E: And a spoon with something on it. . . .
G: Who votes that?
B: All of us? . . . Yeah, all of us. Right, so infants have potato
    race.
C: Write down 6 of us voted for that, 6 out of 6.
B: Ms Robertson's class, potato race . . . we could call it The
    Potato Steam Race. . . .

The tape goes on in much the same vein as this, giving everyone a
fair chance to give their ideas. Morenike, a natural leader, keeps
ushering the rest of the children back to the task. If they go off the
point a little too much, she influences them subtly, not wanting to
appear bossy. Only at one point does she 'take over'. The little girl
who is writing down the proposed races isn't working fast enough and
Morenike takes over without first seeking the consensus of the group.
Apart from that the discussion takes on the guise of a meeting. Votes
are cast and counted as to who agreed with what races to hold. They
decide to look at the infants first and work up. They are well aware of
what younger children are, and are not, capable and above all they
want the day to be fun. The difference between this tape and the
comprehension tape is that the consensus the children are working
towards is one of internal agreement. By that, I mean that they
haven't specifically been asked to write anything down from set
written matter. Therefore they feel more confident in putting their
own opinions forward than, for example, on Tape Two. There they
have a rigid set of written questions to answer and they know that
they have to answer them in an equally rigid written manner. This
decreases their confidence and sets a tone for the conversation, which
is one of tension. Hence, it appears, the freer the structure the more
logical and methodical their talk.
    Constant playback of Tape Four shows me that children are well
able to organize and learn from themselves as well as from the
teacher. By saying this, I don't mean that children should be allowed

complete freedom. They perhaps needed the preceding written comprehension, story, and mathematical work in order to be able to arrive at the stage they were at on Tape Four. On Tape Four, I do not appear to be an authority figure. The conversation doesn't change when I come back into the room. They carry on, involve me in the discussion as an equal and don't look to me to say yes and no to their suggestions. They do that for themselves. What I say doesn't have more importance than their utterances, which is very pleasing.

On reflection, I think all the tapes I have made have shown that children need to feel comfortable and confident in order to increase and value their powers of expression. We, as teachers, can only understand this by listening to the children's talk, either by means of a tape recording or by sitting and listening in the classroom to the wide range of talk in which the children engage. Through listening to how the children work together, I have gained a greater insight into what goes on in my classroom. I have also gained a greater understanding of the tremendous value of talk and its enormous relevance to the learning process.

Part Three

Whole-school Perspectives

Chapter 11

Reorganization and research

John Hickman and Keith Kimberley

In Chapter 4, we outlined the links set up between the school's Language and Learning Committee and a number of outside groups; namely the Newham Talk and Learning Group, the London Association for the Teaching of English (LATE) Talk Working Party, and the Schools' Council Language for Learning Project. The establishment of these links might be read as an indication that at Forest Gate School there was now a group of teachers who were bursting with confidence and would take any opportunity to speak to a group of teachers or write up a set of classroom observations. This is far from the truth. To be sure there were members of the Committee who were beginning to participate in activities beyond the school but this was not from a sense of being expert. To the contrary, two years of investigations and discussions had, paradoxically, made us aware of how little we knew. So, just when it may have looked as if we were confident about the relationship of language and learning and had ideas to share with others, the group became introspective and started to ask some searching questions about what had been achieved and its future direction.

One of the forms that this questioning took was focused around the reading of texts. We thought this was needed in order to shift attention away from individual, first-hand experience; an emphasis which we knew had come to dominate our work. Texts were chosen because they seemed to be able to offer something to everyone on the Committee and each one was presented by a member of the group who gave a synopsis of the main ideas and tried to relate them to the interests of the Committee.

The texts chosen were: *The Language of Text-Books* (Harold Rosen), *Language and the Mind* (Noam Chomsky), *The Logic of Non-Standard English* (William Labov), all in Cashdan and Grugeon (1972); 'The Two Curricula of Schooling' (Chapter 1 of *The Challenge for the Comprehensive School: Culture, Curriculum and*

Community (David Hargreaves, 1982), and a video recording of Jerome Bruner being interviewed by Jonathan Miller.

With the benefit of hindsight, it is easy to see that only a small minority of the group felt this need to look at theory. The majority chose to express their dissent by nonattendance – or silence. (This experiment was going to have to stop if work on language and learning was to survive!) One member, voicing the opinion of many, said that what we were doing had no relevance to what she did in the classroom. It is now however, interesting to speculate, especially given the enthusiasm with which one of the research groups later read texts closely related to their classroom investigations, whether contributory factors to this disaster were the idiosyncratic choice of texts and the unfocused nature of the activity. We are inclined to think that the most important factor was probably the imposition on everybody of a series of academic-style seminars.

These experiences, together with recognition by the Committee that some of us were feeling less involved than others, reinforced a shift in the Committee's way of working. Through the next four terms the research groups, which had been set up by means of the staff survey described in Chapter 4, were to operate autonomously, with occasional reporting back to the full Committee. This change kept work going, despite the difficult times that followed, with the members of each group setting their own agenda, timing, and level of commitment.

Much of the subsequent work of the Committee was diffused, with the meetings of the Committee increasingly tending to provide a forum for discussing activities which were happening elsewhere.

As the research interests of the groups widened, the title Language and Learning was stretched to its limits, raising anxieties in the Committee and the school at large as to whether the Committee had exceeded the limits established in its original, however loose, terms of reference. A suggestion was made that the Committee should rename itself to acknowledge the shifts of concern that had occurred and, while this idea did not receive general support within the group, we became aware of the need to review the relationship of the Committee to broader changes taking place in the school.

It is worth mentioning at this point that the research groups continued working, with greater and lesser degrees of energy, from January 1983 to July 1984. Most of the activity took place in the first year and from January to March 1984 there was the first of a series of periods of industrial action which were to preoccupy teachers until May 1986 (and beyond) at Forest Gate as elsewhere. We are also aware that work done by the research groups had to be fitted around commitments to other school activities such as a school play which dominated the autumn term in 1983. We discuss the likely effects of the imposition of a contract on teachers in the last chapter. Here we only wish to note that the teachers involved in the work which we now describe had to make difficult choices between what they would like to do for themselves, and for the students in their charge, to improve their teaching and what was possible in the context of a long and debilitating struggle with the Government over pay and conditions.

By May 1983 the research groups were beginning to report on their progress. There was general agreement about the value of the type of descriptive research which was being undertaken and each working group made explicit the way it intended to operate. Some question-naires were being used and one group was reviewing statistics, exams, and materials. In all there was a variety of concerns and methods though this is not to suggest that there was no overlap of concerns and common terms of reference. A key effect of the reporting back sessions was to ensure that the thinking of each group informed that of the others. The importance of this will be seen in the three accounts that follow.

Language development outside the English classroom

This group, consisting of Ted Henderson (RS), Jackie Westgarth (HE), Jo Lumsden (English), and Ian Binnie (History), set itself an ambitious task which they quickly realized provided them with difficult problems of organization and focus. This was a common experience for those who undertook investigative work. Even for full-time researchers, the complexity of school settings, and of teacher-student interaction in particular, provides a significant challenge. Here full-time teachers, with many other preoccupations and demands for their attention, were trying to see how far they too could engage in classroom research and find ways of improving their practice. It did not make life any easier for them that many of the models of research known to them were clearly inappropriate to their needs. Additionally, common sense told them that examining one aspect of classroom behaviour or activity would leave unattended layers of complexity of which every practising teacher is aware. There may also have been around a sneaking anxiety that 'professional' researchers would take approaches to data which were more rigorous than those which they might have to adopt.

We make these points to emphasize that teachers need to be quite courageous in undertaking classroom research. They have to keep sight of their wider concerns at the same time tackling something that is manageable, and not be put off by the fear that someone else may have done the thing better already. The group members were, at this stage, in the process of finding their way into a tradition of participant observation and discovering for themselves the constraints as well as the possibilities of being 'teacher as researcher'. Others have documented and discussed this route (for example, Stenhouse, 1975, Richmond, 1982) but each group of teachers, if the undertaking is to be sustained, would seem compelled to establish its own purposes and have a sense of building its own theory.

This research group was remarkable for their decision, despite the bad experiences of the full Committee, to do some reading together and only then to evolve a plan of action. The books which they chose to read were: *Language Teaching and Learning: The Climate for Learning* (Mike Torbe and Peter Medway, 1981), *Language Teaching and Learning: History* (Nick Levine, 1981), *Language Policies in Action* (edited by Mike Torbe, 1980), *Language Across the Curriculum: Four Case Studies* (Irene Robertson, 1980).

One person would read the book and present it to the rest of the group. There would then be a general discussion, generally felt to be particularly useful, in which the group would attempt to relate the ideas to possible areas of research and classroom observation. It may have been important that this activity was initially outward-looking and so removed the threat that could have been experienced if members of the group had been forced to focus on their own practices at too early a stage.

The working relationship established meant that the group was able to keep going in spite of the difficulties that they now encountered. It was decided to focus on talk in the classroom and two observation sheets were devised, one to record student talk and the other to record teacher talk. The sheet relating to student talk was concerned with how much time during the lesson was taken up by student talk and whether it was directed at peers or the teacher. The sheet on teacher talk was rather more detailed and tried to examine the time spent on different kinds of teacher talk: giving instructions, disciplining, encouraging, advising, helping, and questioning. As it was the summer term, it was possible to arrange that each member of the group could observe one of the others on two separate occasions, after the departure of the examination classes. As a consequence, every member of the group had to come to terms with having a 'stranger' in the classroom and particularly one who sat and made notes on what he or she was doing. While those teachers who were fairly used to others popping in and out of their rooms felt reasonably comfortable with the situation, others experienced a considerable amount of stress.

The group met regularly for debriefing sessions and a number of problems were pinpointed:

1.   The observation sheets that had been devised were not a success; there was too much to fill in with the result that insufficient time could be spent observing and reflecting.

2.   In addition to this practical difficulty the categories chosen in constructing the grids were found to be inadequate. Too often they didn't answer the questions the group had wanted to pose.

3.   To observe properly in someone's classroom had begun to look like a full-time job. This sense of inadequacy in the face of the complexities involved was exacerbated by the fact that the exercise, inevitably, had to be low on their day-to-day lists of priorities.

4.   It had proved very difficult to extrapolate information which they could use from the data they had gathered.

So, after much work and thought, the term ended without clear-cut findings from the research they had undertaken.

It would have been very easy for the group to have felt dispirited but they were all positive about their experiences. They thought they had learned a great deal for themselves but had not produced the kind of ideas that could be shown to have direct relevance to other people's practice or to school policy. As they saw it, they had benefited on a much more personal level; they had worked closely across department boundaries and had not only shared some classroom experiences but had also, through contact with alternative ideas and perceptions, had to clarify their own philosophies. When they reported back to the Language and Learning Committee, two of the groups mentioned a gain in personal confidence as a positive outcome; two were reassessing their style of teaching because of their experiences in the group; and all were felt to have been open to the comments made to them. Though in 'research' terms they felt they had failed, they were happy with their involvement in the collaborations since the study and negotiation to set up the activity and the reflection on it afterwards had opened up issues which had hitherto lain dormant or been ignored. On the basis of their report, the Language and Learning Committee concluded that the model being set up by this research group was one worth developing, with more time being found for interdepartmental observation. Two specific areas of investigation were thought desirable. We suggested that attention should be paid to how teaching styles affect response and also to the ways in which different views of what constitutes knowledge influence the success or failure of mixed ability teaching. We did not think their 'failure' to devise methods of analysis which were capable of capturing all the complexities of classroom inter-action should be allowed to discourage them in their enterprise, which seemed to us to be uncovering some of those very complexities.

Race and gender

The investigations undertaken by this group were linked by a shared awareness of the need to identify any forms of racism and sexism that might be built into the curriculum and organization of the school. They started from a recognition that they would need to conduct very specific, precise studies if they were not to fall into the trap of using these terms indiscriminately, a situation which they knew would prove unproductive in convincing people that change was necessary. As a research group of the Language and Learning Committee they hoped to link into, and provide information for, discussions which had been taking place in a variety of forms through the school.

Robin Rice from the Religious Studies Department contributed a review of the sociology and history examination syllabuses with respect to both race and gender. He described the components of each syllabus in detail, showing how, even where there were questions explicitly concerned with issues of race or gender, there could be racist or sexist implications. For example, the A Level Sociology examination which he described was considered to have acceptable questions on gender issues but had very little on racial issues, except for questions in which 'ethnic minorities' were perceived as a problem. Similarly the CSE history examination (1760 to the present day) had had questions on the suffragettes and Elizabeth Fry but no mention of more recent female historical figures, and the questions on Hitler had made no reference to racism.

For this group, Jon McGill did a study of the racial and gender composition of classes taking fifth-year exams. This work complemented the review of examination questions. Among other things, he discovered that at Forest Gate girls were not by and large taking science subjects, that Asian students rarely opted for art, and that students of Asian and Caribbean background appeared to continue their courses right up to the end of the fifth year, non-entries in English and history, for example, being almost entirely white students. Discussions which followed in the group ranged widely and were, at times, tortuous, particularly those on stereotyping. In reporting to the Language and Learning Committee, the group suggested that all teachers needed to investigate the extent to which their perceptions of students' different cultural backgrounds influence their expectations and classroom behaviour.

We should also mention that, in addition to the paper on Language and Race from which we quoted in Chapter 4, Jon McGill also wrote two discussion papers: one entitled *Education for a Multicultural Society* and another *Gender and Education*. Both papers, though not written specifically for them, certainly influenced the thinking of the people working in the Race and Gender research group.

The paper on *Education for a Multicultural Society* was an argument that the school should adopt an explicit policy covering aims, attitudes, and change in the curriculum in response to the multi-faceted nature of the community which the school serves.

> Our pupils are diverse, though in the context of what will be said later about race and class, it is well to remember that they always were. Now the diversity extends into national backgrounds, group experiences and, perhaps most important, their conception of the society in which they now live. To meet this cultural diversity with an improved and more sensitive school response is the challenge offered by multicultural education. Such a response involves not only the content of education but the attitudes and activities of the teachers who, after all, convey most of the messages and meanings.

This statement about the need for Forest Gate School to face up to the changing nature of society was, we think in retrospect, an important base for much of the thinking that was to be developed later both in the staff room and in the Language and Learning Committee. The paper insisted on the need to go beyond bland statements concerning harmony and values and grapple with what needed to be done when racist remarks occurred in the classroom, either as insults or as part of genuine discussion. He argued that teachers must face up to the impact of racism in schools and develop a policy to counteract it. Thinking of this kind was to inform the writing of the Forest Gate Community School Statement which, in 1986, became the school's official, explicit policy (see Chapter 2).

Looking back, we also find his other paper, on *Gender and Education*, fascinating in its scope. Though his initial intention was to look at pastoral provision in the school with relation to issues of gender, he found it necessary to go beyond his reading about counselling and career guidance and propose a wider agenda –

> which encompasses curriculum, open and covert, reading schemes, staff attitudes, LEA hiring policy and the myriad other ways and means of enforcing what is at heart an ideological and class-based situation.

By providing figures on career prospects for men and women teachers, analysing the record of the teacher unions in tackling sexism, and charting a set of historical stages by which sex differentiation has been ascribed to biological imperatives, he contributed to a growing sense of anxiety about the curriculum, pastoral care and discipline, staffing practices and staff relationships, which has continued to resurface in different forms since then.

ESL in the mainstream classroom

We find it interesting to note how different the ways of working of the three research groups turned out. After its first four months together, the English as a Second Language group had established from their investigations that there was a prima facie case for a major policy change in the school. The broad questions with which the group had begun (see Chapter 4) had narrowed to a single question as to whether the school should continue with its traditional model of ESL provision in which teaching was arranged in groups withdrawn from the mainstream curriculum or provide support for second language learners in the context of subject lessons.

The group had set themselves the task of gathering information from the staff as a whole and from ESL students, as well as making their own observations. They had managed to persuade 41 members of the teaching staff to complete a questionnaire on second language learning, finding that 34 of them would regard favourably the opportunity to have ESL support teachers working alongside them in their subject lessons. They also discovered that those surveyed did not always have a strong sense of which students needed support for their English, sometimes failing to distinguish between second-language learners and those with learning difficulties. They had conducted an analysis of the timetables of some first-, second-, and third-year students needing second language support. From this they were able to build a picture of the ways in which the patterns of withdrawal affected the curriculum they experienced. This, together with taped discussions with small groups of students (followed up a year later by individual interviews with the same students), gave them a considerable amount of information about the nature of the students' experience and perceptions. Most startling was the unanimously held belief among the students that they had been singled out for ESL withdrawal classes on the basis of their colour and the reports they gave of victimization and insults from fellow students as a result of having to go to ESL lessons.

The research group wrote up the results of the survey and interviews and this is included, along with their first efforts to look at the practical consequences of ESL support in a subject classroom, as Chapter 13. We think that the story that chapter tells is a very interesting example of how careful gathering of information, combined with a demonstrable concern for the students and a desire to develop a consensus among the teaching staff, can help create structural change in a school. We also note that the conclusions of the research group, and the decision made in the school to reshape ESL provision, took place in advance of policy changes at LEA and national levels.

Shared findings

Suggestions were again made at the beginning of the school year 1984/5 that the Language and Learning Committee should make inputs into staff meetings and make generally available records of past work. Through the history of the Committee this discussion appeared regularly on the agenda but on this occasion it had added force. One reason for this was that the emphasis on small groups working together on the investigations described above had trans-ferred the centre of gravity to the groups, with meetings of the full Committee being needed only for sharing. Another reason lay in the effects on teachers' lives and teaching of the industrial action being taken. This involved 'withdrawal of goodwill' and made it impossible for members of the Committee to take on work which involved meeting outside school hours, even when this also limited their own personal development. All in all we felt that this forced irregularity of meetings of the full Committee had led to a loss of momentum and that a specific focus for the whole group was necessary to generate a new sense of purpose. It was suggested that there should be more sharing and dissemination of ideas and research groups were exhorted to write up their work quickly, and a compilation of past papers was promised for the staff room.

It would, however, be unfortunate to underestimate the value of the processes which the research groups engaged in or to over-estimate the importance of writing up. We do not think the Language and Learning Committee ever resolved its relationship with the staff as a whole. We were never sure of how to present ideas about how children learn to other teachers in ways which wouldn't sound like us telling them how to teach, and we were always conscious that accounts of processes at work in the classroom might sound unconvincing in the formality of a full staff meeting. This said, it seems clear that, in spite of our continued refusal to go public in this direct manner, the ideas of these three research groups did feed into staff-wide discussion. It will be recalled that the whole staff was given an opportunity to join one of these groups and that the reporting-back sessions were similarly open to all. What the Language Development Outside the English Classroom group were doing in their long series of meetings was much discussed, both in the Committee and informally in the staff room. Their programme of reading and observation in each other's classrooms gave a model for such activities and, although they did little writing up other than minutes of their meetings, we do not think this matters. By contrast, the Race and Gender group, which was less tightly-knit, depended on the writing of papers by individuals to help in focusing. The ESL in the Mainstream Classroom group's commitment to policy change meant that information was presented to the whole staff as results of surveys and proposals for action, with the description of classroom processes retreating into the background. The variety of strategies adopted by the groups was, we think, instructive and the lack of a uniform approach to dissemination of ideas and writing up desirable – if unplanned.

The following chapter, which is Nicki Regan's account of following a first-year class through one day, is included because it had a substantial influence on the work of all the research groups. We also think it is full of valuable insights into the ways in which students experience a school and is an activity which all teachers should, at some time, undertake. Chapter 13 documents the work of the ESL research group. Chapter 14 describes the formation of the Educational Support and Development Department and is based on a presentation to the Language and Learning Committee by Jill Wallis and Elaine Mount. By this time Elaine Mount had moved from the English Department to take charge of coordinating the work of the ESD Department. These closely related chapters give a full indication of the way those involved in the support departments were thinking as they began to develop radically different practices from those which had been appropriate for separate ESL and Remedial classes.

Chapter 12

A first-year class through one day

Nicki Regan

During the summer of 1982 a number of members of the Language and Learning Committee planned to follow different groups of students around for a day to help us make some sort of assessment of the school's hidden curriculum. Only Nicki Regan managed to do this, being so thorough that she spent break time and lunch time with her chosen group.

In the summer term of 1982, I spent one Friday as a pupil with Form 1Y, one of six classes of about 24 pupils of mixed ability in the first year. My aim was two fold. Firstly to discover the kinds of language pupils are exposed to and the linguistic demands made on them during an 'average' day at Forest Gate School. Secondly, in a more general sense, I wanted to experience Forest Gate School as a pupil instead of as a teacher.

I feel it should be said at this stage, although I will expand on this later, that due to the fact that 1Y was a class that I knew well because I teach them and also because being first years they lack certain inhibitions of older classes, I did quite genuinely feel that I was a pupil for that day because I was accepted so readily by the children. I am not sure that this would have been so easy with an older, unknown set of pupils.

What follows is a record of my observations of my day as a pupil. My account falls into two parts; firstly, a résumé of each lesson, and secondly, more general comments about my experience.

My day began at 8.50 a.m. when I lined up outside the class room for registration. The atmosphere during registration was informal, talk between us being anecdotal about teachers, lessons, friends, etc. The only direct contact between pupil and teacher was in answer to the register and also on one occasion when two boys approached the teacher, who also taught them geography, to discuss some work.

At the bell we went to French and lined up outside. The aim of the French lesson was to practise language needed to buy bread in

103

preparation for 1Y's trip to Boulogne. Terms familiar to the pupils were spoken in French, new phrases were explained in both French and English and printed on the blackboard as well. After an introduction, the class was divided into small groups of their own choice to practise buying bread, with the help of cards, each one showing a different type of bread with the French word printed below the picture.

Most groups included children of varying abilities although mine consisted of three girls, all able and highly motivated. Given the make-up of the group, I felt I certainly learnt a lot more by taking an active role and practising the language than I would have done by sitting and listening or working alone on prescribed written tasks. However, other groups, in particular one consisting of four boys, were less involved and I questioned how much I would have benefited from group work in this situation. Certainly very little if I too had been uninterested and, if I had been motivated, I would not have had the courage to persuade the others to work.

To a great extent I was unable to participate in the second lesson, music, as I had been absent previously for the exam. The class sat in pairs, again of their own choice, exam papers were returned, marked together in class and final marks were called out to the teacher. I wondered how I would have felt about calling out my mark if it had been low.

For the last five minutes of the lesson, the class prepared to sing a song they'd learnt in a previous lesson from a song book. This I felt, would have demanded a great deal of pupils as the task involved:

(a) An ability to read the lyrics.
(b) An ability to understand the specialized language of music symbols.
(c) An ability to coordinate notes and lyrics during the song.

Unlike lunchtime, which I'll describe later, I enjoyed break time. I attached myself to two girls, Kirti and Karen, with whom in fact I spent most of my free time. We went firstly to the kitchen to buy cake and coffee and then sheltered from the rain under 'the bridge' linking the playground with the main school and a favourite meeting place. We chatted until the end of break, talk again being anecdotal.

A double lesson of geography followed this. Again the pupils sat in pairs of their own choice and the lesson was teacher directed on the subject of weather stations. The format of the lesson was as follows:

1. A recap on the previous lesson (obviously I was at a disadvantage here.)
2. A diagram of a thermometer was distributed to the class. The

teacher then explained how it worked and simple, related tasks were then set.

3. A plan of fictitious school grounds with eight possible positions for a weather station, labelled A-H, and a set of instructions were handed out to the class. Again, the teacher talked these through and the class was then asked to determine the best position for a weather station, working alone.

There was obviously a fair amount of specialized language involved in this lesson; words such as 'thermometer', 'anemometer' and 'pin' spring to mind. A few were completely new to me or certainly unfamiliar in their specialized, geographical sense of the word though all were explained by the teacher and my understanding of them was also enhanced by reference to the labelled diagram.

I was surprised by the confidence the pupils showed in this lesson to ask questions when they did not understand. This occurred far more frequently in geography than in other lessons I witnessed that day and such questions also came from a larger proportion of the class. Whilst in other lessons it tended to be always the same group of more able pupils who articulated their queries, the less able and/or the more reserved members of the class also contributed in geography and such questions were always responded to by the teacher.

Various tentative conclusions could perhaps be drawn from this example and, whilst obviously open to debate, it is worth, I feel, posing them. I feel perhaps that there is a correlation between level of ability and level of confidence. This is, of course, not a hard and fast rule and we can all hopefully immediately think of a large number of exceptions from our own teaching experience. Nevertheless, I feel that often the labelling process that goes on in most classrooms, however subtle, is obviously a prime indicator of the child's self-image and, therefore, either an aid or an impediment to understanding and confidence.

The fact that such a pattern is inconsistent in some lessons where pupils seem more willing to voice their uncertainties, also begs the question of why this is the case. I feel here that the crux of the matter lies in the confidence a pupil has in his or her teacher. The fact that the geography teacher responded to every question asked, always in a tone of voice that indicated encouragement and praise for the pupil's initiative, helped the children to recognize their own worth and feel secure in voicing queries as well as statements.

My own inhibitions about doing this were due to the fact that I was new to the class and somewhat of an oddity given my usual role as teacher. Furthermore, I was unsure of the way the teacher would react to my intervention; would it have been welcomed or treated as an unnecessary intrusion? For a pupil surely such confidence only emerges gradually as a trusting relationship develops between teacher and pupil. This is perhaps an argument for the same teacher following one class up through the school, perhaps increased here by the fact that the teacher was also 1Y's form tutor and thus met the class in more informal situations as well.

As I said previously, this particular geography lesson consisted of three sections. During the unit on the thermometer, I worked in a pair with a girl called Cindy, a very able pupil who explained the work to me carefully. As I had failed to understand a lot of what the teacher had said in his initial talk on this subject, Cindy's guidance was invaluable. Nevertheless, I still failed to understand completely and, though my work was checked by the teacher to ensure that I had worked the answers out correctly, the fact that he had twenty-four other pupils to attend to, meant that he had insufficient time to explain to me personally the cause of my mistakes. Because I was motivated enough to then seek further advice from two other pupils, I finally reached a full understanding of the thermometer. If, however, pupils like myself had not been sufficiently motivated to ask for help, their degree of understanding would presumably have been limited.

During the work on weather stations, I was at an immediate disadvantage because I had been absent from the previous lesson when a more detailed study of the function and mechanics of a weather station had been studied. As a result, I found this section of the lesson particularly difficult. Pupils needed the following skills for this unit of work:

1. An ability to interpret the map.
2. An ability to read and understand instructions (especially technical language).
3. An ability to relate instructions to the map.

We worked alone on this occasion. Whilst trying to work out correct answers, I overhead a lot of pupils muttering 'position H' and was tempted to follow the majority without thinking through the implications. To be independent, I opted finally for position B, though still without enough careful thought.

The teacher checked our final answers by calling out each location in alphabetical order and asking pupils to raise their hands to indicate their decision. I was asked to justify my decision and in so doing realized why location B would have been unsuitable. Had I not been asked to do this, however, I would not have understood my mistake. As this must have been true for a good percentage of the class, I wonder whether discussion would not have been better here where a more reasoned response would have been demanded of pupils initially.

During this unit of work, I also took particular notice of a pupil named Rajwant who was sitting close to me. Rajwant is a girl for whom English is a second language. In her English lessons she sometimes experienced difficulty in understanding certain aspects of the work and also struggled to communicate her ideas fluently, particularly in writing, lacking the necessary language and some of the basic technical skills.

She had made no attempt to work out the location for the weather station due, I feel, to a lack of understanding as she normally worked very conscientiously when she did comprehend the task. When asked at the end to indicate her choice, however, she selected the correct position of H. Though I may of course be wrong, I feel that her correct answer, which should in theory indicate understanding, was in fact, (a) to the fact that like me she had overheard a lot of the 'reliable sources' voicing H, and (b) to the fact that alphabetically H was the last possible option and she had decided to wait as long as possible before raising her hand.

Thus, although Rajwant, and presumably other pupils as well, 'appeared' to have learnt from this geography lesson, it is possible that she had gained nothing at all and, furthermore, that this would never be detected. One should also bear in mind that this was in a lesson with a well-organized and understanding teacher.

In the afternoon, the pupils were separated for PE; the boys being taken by the two male members of the department; the girls by the female staff. Both groups were joined by pupils from other first year classes as is customary for this subject. Due to the bad weather, the lesson was held indoors and after changing into PE kit in the changing rooms, the lesson began with a warm-up game with a large element of 'fun' attached to it to involve everyone and reduce the self-consciousness obviously felt by some pupils.

This was followed by a game of indoor cricket, each team chosen by a team captain, carefully selected by the teacher from amongst the less 'popular' members of the class who might otherwise have faced the embarrassment of being chosen last for a team. This selection process brought back memories of my own school days when being neither athletic, nor a dominant member of the class, I would cringe with embarrassment as I waited to be picked.

During the actual game, I was also constantly aware, as I imagine some of the other pupils must have been, that I was under constant observation as people watched me make a fool of myself. A practical subject such as PE can be altogether more daunting for someone lacking in self-confidence than a formal classroom lesson which provides the security of 'hiding behind the desk'.

Unlike other lessons I witnessed during the day, PE demanded far less formal language. Each activity was preceded by brief instructions from the teacher which involved some technical, specialized vocabulary, but for the main part, the language consisted of brief interchanges to encourage or advise from teacher to pupil or pupil to pupil with very little communication on this occasion between teacher and individual pupil. Much spoken communication was substituted with body language where pupils were corrected or praised by means of gesture and demonstration. Throughout the lesson, for example, the teacher would interrupt periodically to correct or reinforce some point, using the pupils themselves as agents in the demonstration. This form of non-verbal communication is probably more apparent in this and other practical subjects than in other areas of the curriculum.

Mathematics was the only subject in Forest Gate School, at that time, where the first years did not remain in their mixed-ability tutor group but were streamed immediately upon entry to the school by means of a test. I had decided previously that for my final lesson of the day, I would accompany pupils who have learning difficulties in this subject.

The arguments for and against streaming continue to be debated and do not need to be reiterated here. In the light of my experience with 1Y, however, I would strongly disagree with anyone who dared to claim that streaming goes unnoticed by the children, who without a doubt attribute a hierarchical status to it. Throughout the day, I was continually asked by the children which maths class I would be attending and when I replied that I would be going to Mr Lane's lesson, I was informed that this was 'the bottom group'. Whilst one would hope that as teachers we would never refer to streamed classes in such overt terms as 'top' or 'bottom' group, it is nevertheless clear that here again pupils learn through implication to class themselves as part of a particular ability grouping.

At that time, support teaching within the mainstream classroom was in its early stages at Forest Gate School, most pupils needing extra help being withdrawn from lessons to the Remedial or ESL Department. Mathematics was an exception where support teaching was available for less able pupils who followed the Kent Mathematical Scheme of individualized learning.

In the lesson I attended, the pupils were already at very different stages on their programme of work and there was no focal start to the lesson. Each pupil had already previously received a 'matrix' of assignments – a timetable of sequential tasks to be accomplished from a series of self-explanatory cards. At the beginning of the lesson, each pupil had collected the material he or she needed to continue on this programme of work. After each task, the pupils' work was marked by the teacher before they could move on to the next stage.

It appeared to me that the nature of the work, where pupils were at very different stages, did not allow for much collaboration amongst the children. On the other hand, being a small group with two members of staff, there was much more individual contact between pupil and teacher than in other lessons that day.

Having been absent from previous lessons, and being unaware of the process leading up to or following the pupil's current matrix of work, I am of course ill-equipped to assess the true value of the mathematics lesson I experienced as a pupil. However, having been assigned my own matrix of work, I questioned how much I would have learnt if I had found the tasks difficult for it appeared rather to me that my success depended upon my ability to work out the 'key' to solving the task on the card. Having done this I was able to accomplish the work in this narrow context but I wondered whether I would have been able to relate this to similar mathematical problems in a wider context.

Thus far, I have concentrated on a breakdown of the lessons in which 1Y and I participated. To move on, I wish now to focus firstly on one particular member of 1Y and lastly to give a more general overview of my impressions of Forest Gate School as a pupil.

Sharmin, for whom English was a second language, had great language difficulties both orally and especially in written work. Having taught her throughout her first year, I had also come to realize the social problems she faced within the class, where she was a noticeable outsider, isolated from the majority of the group. Sometimes she sat completely alone when present in lessons, sometimes she was joined by two other girls who made a conscious effort to include her in their work and help her as much as possible. One of these girls was Rajwant, the other Karen. Due to the fact that in several subjects Sharmin was withdrawn for at least part of the timetable, she missed a lot of work and was at a complete loss when returning to the lesson. Not being present with the rest of the class for much of the time, also meant that she had never established herself within a particular social group and hence, certainly in English, was often deprived of the support from her peers, something experienced by other members of the class which would have been of particular value to Sharmin.

Whilst clearly already at a great disadvantage, I found to my horror, that even outside lesson time, Sharmin remained isolated. Unlike other pupils who, if isolated within their form class, have their own group of friends drawn from other form or year groups, she appeared to have none. Thus, if the day that I spent with 1Y may be considered typical, her experience of school was one of almost total isolation, depriving her of any opportunity to socialize with others, to seek help with work and to develop her English language skills; the last fact perhaps being the most worrying.

During morning registration Sharmin spoke to no one. Whilst

hovering on the edge of a group, she was never invited to join in. Having been withdrawn for the first two lessons, she once again joined the rest of the class at break time. On this occasion, she approached the group that I was with in the playground but once again was ignored and eventually wandered off on her own. Again being withdrawn for the next two lessons, Sharmin faced similar rejection during lunch time which she once again spent alone.

Against such a backcloth, the change that occurred in Sharmin during the afternoon was extremely noticeable. As a member of the maths group which I had chosen to join, she was obviously delighted that I would be attending this lesson and voiced on several occasions the fact that I was going to her maths class. Quite clearly she felt, presumably for the first time that day, that she was important and was being recognized. As a result, I was taken under her wing. During PE she remained close to me throughout the lesson. She invited me to sit next to her in maths and enjoyed the opportunity of explaining the work to me, recognizing that I was at a disadvantage and that for once she was in the stronger position, able to share her knowledge with someone who did not understand. Sharmin's drastic change in response to recognition is perhaps one of the most important things to emerge from that day.

I mention Sharmin in particular, because I feel that once again, this example raises several issues. Firstly, as teachers, most of us would like to feel that we know our pupils well, indeed this is surely an important factor if we are really to assist pupils in their development while at school. Although a teacher who works with a group of children regularly over a period of time, should know each child well academically, a knowledge of them in other ways (home background, socially, etc.) is not so immediately apparent and sometimes, as in my own perception of Sharmin, relies on assumptions rather than facts.

It was only because I spent one day following pupils more closely through their life in school, that I discovered the isolation that I am assuming Sharmin experienced every day. As far as I know, no other member of staff was aware of this either. This raises the question of how many other pupils with whom we come into contact, experience difficulties of whatever kind in school, obviously having a detrimental effect on their learning, of which teachers are never aware.

Secondly, this example raises the question of how useful the practice of withdrawing pupils from the mainstream classroom for additional support work can be. As Forest Gate School's research work into traditional ESL provision verifies, adverse effects on such pupils often far outweigh any beneficial effects.

Finally, my day with 1Y provided me with the opportunity to assess Forest Gate School more generally through the eyes of a pupil. Such an experience left me with a very different and rather disturbing impression to the one I had gained as a teacher.

Most noticeably, I was struck by the lack of contact I, as a pupil, had with teachers that day. I had spoken to a teacher directly only during registration as I responded to my name in the register and in geography. As I have outlined previously the only really individual attention I received was during maths, made possible by the smaller class size and extra member of staff; a situation available to only a minority of pupils at that time. One might assume from this that the same lack of contact might be experienced by other pupils, something which we as teachers perhaps need to monitor more closely if we are to ensure that it is not only the more articulate or 'disruptive' members of the class who demand and gain the attention of their teachers.

It also became clear to me how, unconsciously, teachers may isolate themselves from pupils outside lesson time as well. The staff room at Forest Gate School, positioned on the top floor of a three-storey building, was perhaps designed thus to allow staff to enjoy their free lessons and break time in peace and to discourage pupil callers who are still often regarded as an unnecessary intrusion.

As a pupil, the staff room became a mysterious room at the top of the school which I, like many other pupils, had no cause to visit and which, away from the main thoroughfare of the school, isolated me further from teachers. When we ask pupils to visit the staff room for whatever reason and receive a negative response as they claim that they do not know where it is, we should perhaps regard their ignorance with concern rather than annoyance. In passing, perhaps we should also question, certainly at Forest Gate School, the justification for placing many of the offices belonging to pastoral staff and senior teachers in similarly inaccessible regions of the school.

Regulations governing pupil activity during break and lunch time at Forest Gate School, complete the pattern of segregating staff from pupils. Though enjoyable, I outline below the process whereby pupils are excluded from the building during break time. Far less pleasant are the lunch time rules which demand a similar absence of children from school. Whilst for staff, a break of 1 hour 25 minutes might be a welcome opportunity to attend meetings, catch up on marking or simply relax in the warmth of the school building, my reaction as a pupil, and that of many children I talked to that lunch time and since, was one of resentment that I was forced outside for such a long period of time whilst watching staff walk freely into the building.*

---

* Since this was written the school has been opened up at break time and, when the weather is bad, at lunch time also.

On the day I spent with 1Y, it rained persistently and was also quite cold. Having bought a hot dog from the burger van outside school, Karen, Kirti and myself managed to sneak into the girls' cloakroom to eat it! Braving the elements for a trip to the sweet shop, we were refused re-entry by the dinner ladies on our return and so opted to stand under the shelter of the main gate for the remaining part of lunch time. Killing three quarters of an hour in these conditions is boring and whilst it could be argued that I might have enjoyed the lunch time more if I had been with my friends as many of the pupils were, my resentment at being excluded from the building would have remained the same.

For all but a few pupils who might participate in a lunch time club, the same regulations would have applied, once again increasing the sense of isolation felt by pupils towards their school and teachers.

Thus my general impression of Forest Gate School as a pupil, was that of a rather large, cold and unfriendly institution. I was accepted very readily and genuinely as a pupil by all but a few of 1Y and thus felt I witnessed school quite successfully from a pupil's point of view. Only in social terms, where I was not with my peers and was not in reality part of a friendship group, did I feel excluded and as a result, quite relieved to return to the fortress at the top of the school at the end of the day. Perhaps, even here, my experience was similar to that of other pupils, of Sharmin in particular, and of other children during their first days at Forest Gate School or of those who enter the school late and join a class which has already established itself socially.

I feel that this experience was invaluable and afforded me an insight into life at school as a pupil which I could not have gained in any other way, and which can enable us, as teachers, to understand better the experiences and needs of our pupils. For others who may wish to attempt a similar experiment in their own school, I include below, in conclusion, a few comments which might be useful considerations for future practice:

(a) In terms of adopting the role of a pupil, I feel perhaps that this might be achieved more successfully with a younger class who may accept more readily than older pupils the change from the teacher role.

(b) The experiment might also be of greater benefit if executed by a teacher with a class which he or she has taught for a while, enabling the teacher to compare more effectively the pupils' responses to such things as social groupings, class participation and so on.

(c) As a follow up, it would be valuable to pursue the experiment with each year group within the school to compare the shifting demands and expectations made of pupils. Furthermore,

112

perhaps to repeat the experiment with the same class as they move up the school would prove a very worthwhile exercise.

(d) Spending the whole day with pupils through their break and lunch times, also provides one with a wider picture of their life at school and enables one to gain an insight into the hidden curriculum of the school, a very important but often difficult aspect to assess.

Chapter 13

Support for second language learning

Wendy Parmley and Pat Roberts

In this chapter, Wendy Parmley and Pat Roberts report on work done by a sub-group of the Language and Learning Committee, which examined the way in which the school supported second language learners. The research conducted by the group was a starting point in bringing about a change from a withdrawal system to the provision of support in the mainstream classroom.

The starting-point for the research which we have described here was a deepening sense of unease shared by a number of teachers that pupils who were withdrawn from mainstream classes to be given help with second language learning were thereby suffering both academically and socially. At that time (1981-2), ESL pupils were grouped according to linguistic achievement rather than age and, as a consequence of this grouping and the withdrawal system, they were missing a wide variety of subject lessons.

Five teachers joined together to form the research group. Their experiences ranged from Scale 1 to deputy head level and a number of subject areas were represented: English, ESL, French, home economics, sociology and, latterly, maths. There had already been liaison between some of these teachers with regard to pupils for whom English is a second language and, strangely enough, all of those concerned had worked together at parent-teacher functions. A camaraderie which pervaded the group made working together enjoyable.

Aims of the research

At the outset of the research we aimed to find out:

1. The effect of existing ESL provision on:
    (a) the pupil,

114

    (b)   subject staff attitudes towards that pupil.
2. The effect of subject-based ESL support.
    (At that time such support occurred in only one lesson a week, a second-year mixed-ability geography set.)
3. The educational advantages and disadvantages of ESL being taught in a withdrawal situation.
4. The needs of the mainstream teacher in providing for a pupil for whom English is a second language.

The most pressing issue was to examine the effects of traditional ESL provision (Aim 1). The questionnaire was devised and distributed via heads of department to every member of staff. We wished to gain the maximum feed-back possible and felt that by formalizing the procedure, most status would be ascribed to the research. Out of 63 questionnaires issued, 42 were returned.

Staff questionnaire

1. Could you please list the names of any pupils you teach in the mainstream class who have ESL difficulties. We would also like to know their teaching groups and the subject taught.

2. If staffing permitted, would you like an ESL teacher to accompany ESL pupils to your lessons

    (a)   all the time?
    (b)   at certain times?
    (c)   never?

3. Do you on occasions prepare simplified work or worksheets for ESL pupils who attend your lessons?

4. Would you like the cooperation of ESL staff in preparing. simplified work or worksheets?

5. In your opinion, are there disadvantages of having ESL pupils in the mainstream class from the point of view of:

    (a)   the rest of the class?
    (b)   the teacher?
    (c)   the ESL pupil him/herself?

If yes to any of these, please give reasons and examples if possible.

6. In your opinion, are there advantages to having ESL pupils in the mainstream class:

    (a)   for the rest of the class?

(b) for the teacher?

(c) for the ESL pupil him/herself?

Please give reasons and examples if possible.

7. Sometimes it is necessary to withdraw an ESL pupil for extra intensive teaching to correct particular problems. What are your feelings about the pupil missing some or all of your lessons?

8. How difficult or easy is it to re-introduce the ESL pupil to your lessons if he/she has missed:

(a) one out of the weekly quota of lessons?

(b) a whole term?

(c) a whole year?

9. Do you have any other comments on the matter?

Although most of the findings from teachers' responses to the questionnaire were predictable, some were a cause for concern. In response to Question 1, teachers named more than twice as many pupils in the first year whom they believed had ESL difficulties than those, who in reality, did. The naming of ESL pupils in other years was more accurate but it was evident that there was a little confusion in some teachers' analyses of the pupils' individual difficulties and a number of the names given were of pupils for whom English is the only language.

Eighty per cent of teachers who answered the questionnaire said they would like ESL teachers in their classrooms if staffing permitted and the majority wished this to be at certain times as opposed to all the time. The crucial need for consultation with subject staff before the lesson was stressed and it was hoped that the ESL teacher would display a sensitivity towards the aims of the subject teacher. In answer to Question 3, the majority of teachers said they did not prepare special worksheets for ESL pupils. Reasons given were the time factor involved, a fear that a 'mini-tripartite' situation might be created by the existence of worksheets specially prepared for ESL pupils and thirdly, many teachers felt they 'lacked expertise'. Leading on from this response, 66 per cent of those teachers who answered said they would like help in preparing such worksheets.

In answer to Questions 5 & 6, most teachers thought there were no disadvantages to the rest of the class in having an ESL pupil present and indeed, there were positive advantages. For example, teachers stated that the presence of ESL pupils gives rise to other pupils being able to appreciate the value of languages other than English; it gives all pupils the chance to help one another and to have their views enriched by learning in a multicultural situation. For the subject teacher, the advantages are that their sensitivity is highlighted, their attention is focused on the problem and complexities of the language they use and the difficulties of coping with a pupil who has been withdrawn from their subject are avoided. Only three teachers thought it was not advantageous to the ESL pupil to be in the mainstream classroom. The main disadvantage was when an ESL pupil returned to the mainstream after withdrawal lessons. It was felt that this sometimes slowed down the progress of the rest of the class and that teachers lacked the expertise and/or time to deal effectively with such pupils.

Replies to Question 7 were varied. Forty-three per cent of teachers were positively against ESL pupils being withdrawn from their lessons. Twenty-six per cent said they were not against and 31 per cent had mixed feelings. It was evident that teachers of subjects which are topic-based were open to negotiation whereas teachers of sequential subjects were definitely not! It was commented that, 'Withdrawal to correct one problem causes others'. Answers to Question 8 reflected those opinions expressed in response to Question 7.

As a result of this questionnaire, the ESL department has made available more detailed lists of those pupils who are in receipt of ESL support. The Educational Support and Development (ESD) Department has done so similarly. Since September 1982 ESL support in the mainstream has been gradually implemented so that now many ESL pupils are never withdrawn. The responses to this questionnaire were used as a starting point in this venture. It is the group's intention to requestion staff now that ESL support work has been established in the mainstream classroom.

Shortly after the issue of the questionnaire to teachers, the group took upon themselves the task of observing a first-year class in which there were a high percentage of pupils for whom English is a second language. Our aims were twofold: first we wanted to find out how an ESL pupil copes academically in a large class; and secondly we wanted to find out how an ESL pupil copes socially with the consequences of being taken out of a variety of lessons. Much time was spent in devising a check list for the observation of ESL pupils in mainstream classes but when we used these the results were not as revealing as we had expected. The check list was as follows:

Check list for observation

1. Where is the pupil seated in relation to the teacher?

2. Can the pupil easily see visual aids or hear tapes, etc?

3. Does the pupil have to share a text book?

4. Is the pupil seated (a) in isolation?
   (b) in an evidently ESL group?
   (c) with an able friend?
   (d) with a friend who has learning problems?
   (e) with an able peer (chosen by teacher)?
   (f) otherwise?

   What is the effect of this seating?

5. During the lesson presentation does the pupil actively take part by asking/answering questions?

6. If so, what is the attitude of (a) the teacher?
   (b) the rest of the class?

7. How long does the teacher spend on presentation:
   (a) verbally, (b) in written form, (c) with use of visual aids?

8. Which way best suits ESL pupils? (Why?)

9. If the ESL pupil doesn't actively take part, is he/she paying attention or has he/she 'switched off'?

10. How does the ESL pupil respond if the teacher deliberately asks her/him a question?

11. If the pupil has 'switched off' did this happen at the beginning or at a moment when the content (either for linguistic or academic reasons) became too difficult?

12. Generally speaking, is the lesson content for the class
    (a) too high, (b) too low, (c) just right?

13. Are learning difficulties (if any) for the ESL pupil caused by:
    (a) the language of the teacher and text book being too complicated, (b) the concepts involved in the lesson being beyond the pupil's comprehension (even if MT were used)?

14. When difficulties occur does the pupil ask:
    (a) the teacher, (b) another pupil, (c) pupil with same MT?

15. If the MT is spoken what is the reaction of the (a) rest of the class (b) teacher?

16. In group work activities with whom does the ESL pupil tend to work if he/she can choose where they go?

17. How does the ESL pupil's understanding and production of work compare with the rest of the class?

18. If the ESL pupil is achieving in this lesson, why do you think this is?

19. Are worksheets specially prepared for the ESL pupil?

20. If so, what effect does this pupil's different treatment cause to the pupil in question? Do other pupils show interest in the worksheet?

21. What scope in written work is the ESL pupil given to answer in their own words – or are questions structured?

22. If you were this ESL pupil, would you feel at ease? Why/why not?

It was found that ESL pupils appeared to be coping as well as their contemporaries and that it was the pupils' own individual dispositions and academic abilities which appeared to either hinder or help their learning. Consequently, it was felt that although it had been interesting to observe a group of ESL pupils in the mainstream classroom, and to find the way in which they functioned reassuring, no conclusions could be drawn. The exercise did, however, reveal that at some subject lessons only half the class was present, the other half having been withdrawn for either ESL or reading lessons.

The research group has investigated pupil attitudes so far on two occasions; once in spring 1983 and a year later when the same pupils were re-interviewed. First of all, ESL pupils from the first, third and fifth years were interviewed in small groups of six to eight and the findings were taped but as we believed some pupils had been influenced by their peers' responses, when we later re-interviewed these pupils, they were seen individually. The aim of the interviewing was to find out what pupils experienced at school by having ESL lessons in a withdrawal situation. The questions asked in a group situation were:

Pupil questionnaire

1. Which subject do you think is most popular among your year?
2. Which subject do you think is most use to you?
3. Do you wish you were better at any subject?
4. How many people do you know who go to German lessons?
5. Would you like to learn German?
6. What do you learn in Special English?
7. Do you know anyone who goes for reading lessons?
8. What do people think about people who go for reading?
9. If you could drop one subject, what would it be?
10. If you could add one subject, what would it be?
11. What do you wish you were better at?

119

12.   What do people in your class say about people who go to Special English?
13.   Do your parents want you to have Special English?
14.   How many lessons did you miss last year in order to have Special English?
15.   This year, is it difficult to catch up?
16.   Whom do you speak to in your own language at school?
17.   Do other people think you are clever to be able to speak two languages?
18.   What kind of mistakes do you make in English?
19.   Do you think your subject teachers understand why you make these mistakes?
20.   Which is your best subject?
21.   What career do you want to aim for?

Questions 4 and 5 were included because German is offered in the third year to those pupils who achieve high marks in French during the second year. There is the opportunity for only 30 pupils to study this language and owing to the process of selection to gain a place in the class, the subject has high status. Questions 16 and 17 were included as a matter of interest.

After collating the responses, six main points emerged:

Results of questionnaire

1.   ESL pupils value maths and science highly. The arts appeared to have low status. It is possible that parental expectations encroach on a child's perception of particular subjects.
2.   Most ESL pupils find maths and science difficult and desire to be better at these.
3.   Most ESL pupils said they did not enjoy maths or science but few mentioned the Arts as being enjoyable, either.
4.   The majority of ESL pupils in the first and third years felt that they had been singled out because of their racial background to attend ESL lessons. One pupil remarked, 'it's because we's black, Miss, isn't it?' Few pupils saw the reason for their attendance in terms of being helped with their English.
5.   Most ESL pupils experience some kind of victimization from their peers at having to attend a withdrawal ESL lesson. This, it was felt, mellowed into sympathy or a kind of understanding once pupils reached the sixth form.
6.   The older the ESL pupil, the more he/she saw English as 'the key to success' in all areas of the curriculum and in the outside world.

From that time on, ESL lessons in a withdrawal situation became fewer as ESL support work in the mainstream was increased.

Pupil attitude survey

The next survey which the group carried out sought to discover pupil attitudes towards ESL support in mainstream classes. When pupils were seen individually, they were asked:

Think about how you are at school this year – since September,
Now
1.   Which subject do you think you've made the most progress in since September?
2.   Do you ever have two teachers in one lesson now?
If Yes
2A.   Do you find you get on better if there are two teachers?
3.   Have you made any new friends this year?
If Yes
3A.   Why do you think you have?
4.   Do you have Special English in R3?
If Yes
4A.   Why do you have it?
4B.   What do you think about it?
If No
4C.   Do you wish you had lessons in R3?
Now
Think about how you were at school last year – before the summer holiday.
5.   Did you miss any lessons last year to have Reading or Special English?
If Yes
5A.   Which subject was that?
      How are you managing this year in that subject?
6.   Did you like school better *last* year?
PROBE
Why is that?
Now for some general questions
Which subject do you enjoy most?
Is there any subject you wish you didn't have to do?
Which subject is easiest for you?
Which subject do you find hardest?
Which subject would you most like to be better at?

Eighteen pupils were interviewed from the then years two, four and six. Some pupils had left school since the original group interviews. It was felt that the second survey taken encompassed a sample which was too small and varied to be significant but nevertheless it proved that 'the quality of life' for an ESL pupil has, thankfully, improved.

Conclusions from attitude survey

From the second survey, certain points are worthy of note:

1. The majority of pupils felt they had made progress and in particular in maths, English, and history.
2. The majority had experienced support from ESL teachers in the mainstream classroom and some pupils received support in three subjects.
3. Most pupils felt they got on better with two teachers in the classroom although one said he got confused.
4. Most pupils had made new friends during the year. Two pupils had been put in new option groups. Two felt they had received more help from peers by being present in the mainstream and one pupil mentioned their own personal change and development.
5. About half the group interviewed still received some ESL support in a withdrawal lesson but pupils' perceptions of why they received such lessons were greatly improved. A number said they had such lessons to make their English better and to help them cope in other subjects and one person had requested withdrawal lessons. Three pupils said they did not know why they went to ESL lessons but this time, no-one said they felt it was because of their racial background.
6. Attitudes towards attendance at ESL withdrawal lessons varied from being, 'Alright really', and, 'We learn all sorts of things – it's nice' to, 'I don't like it because people say things' and, 'I miss Drama, I wish I didn't'.
7. Although pupils had missed lessons during the previous year to attend withdrawal classes, most thought they were coping despite experiencing some difficulties.
8. Most pupils still found maths to be the hardest subject, and this was the subject which they most desired to be better at. However, top of the list for enjoyment was English and a significant number now found it to be easier.
9. The majority said they preferred school since the change in the workings of the ESL department. The reasons varied from, 'I have more friends now,' and 'I get more help,' to the fact that they had a new teacher or just simply that life at school is, in general, more fun.

Over the past three years the ESL group has worked towards fulfilling its four original aims, two of which have been achieved to a certain extent. Investigations towards fulfilling Aim 1 have been completed and the social aspects of Aim 2 have been discovered.

Since beginning our work, the ESL group has decided that it should be the brief of the ESL Department to investigate Aim 3. In our plans for the future, we hope to research ways of meeting our fourth aim since we believe that meeting the needs of the mainstream teacher in coping with ESL pupils in their classes is of top priority if we are to suggest ways of enhancing ESL pupils' academic improvement.

It is our intention to carry on monitoring the progress of the ESL pupil in the mainstream class. It has been suggested that we do three case studies of particular pupils, one in the present upper-sixth who coped with learning English as a second language purely in withdrawal lessons; one present fifth-year pupil who has experienced ESL in both withdrawal and support situations; and one second year pupil who has received ESL help purely in the mainstream class. Discussions are already under way about how to fulfil these aims and a new cycle of research is about to commence.

Chapter 14

Support for students with learning difficulties

Elaine Mount

In this chapter, Elaine Mount describes the moves by which the school changed its thinking and structures with relation to provision for students with learning difficulties and discusses the policy and practice needed for a positive approach to working with mainstream teachers across the curriculum.

Historically, secondary schools have been organized to cater mainly for average and above-average pupils and struggled to meet the needs of a number of pupils who may not achieve academic success. The problems of getting appropriate provision in meeting these needs has been aggravated by fragmented timetables, pupils having fleeting contact with a large number of subject teachers, the constant pressure of tests and examinations, the difficulty in understanding subject content, and, sometimes, the formal and inflexible class teaching of many teachers.

The Forest Gate School Remedial and ESL departments had a traditional role in catering solely for pupils with language and learning difficulties through special approaches, methods and techniques. These techniques were supposedly not available to, or within the range of, the subject teacher. The new intake pupils were given Daniels and Diack Standard Reading Test Number 12 at their junior schools. There was little effort at continuity, or familiarization of incoming pupils with Forest Gate staff. On arrival, the whole year-group was retested, this time on the Holborn Reading Scale and those pupils scoring a reading age of ten, or below, were considered 'remedial' pupils and thus withdrawn for one, two, or three lessons per week. They were taught in groups on phonic-based reading schemes. This system was undesirable for a number of reasons:

1. A very large number of pupils from the first and second year were missing mainstream lessons, indeed some second-year pupils had never attended RE lessons for example.

2. Some less able fourth- and fifth-year pupils were persuaded to take a 'reading option'; being denied the opportunity of following a full option programme with examination opportunities.

3. Teachers were becoming increasingly dissatisfied with the problems caused by pupils missing half of their lessons or not having the opportunity to attend a subject area at all.

4. Many pupils for whom English was a second language who were withdrawn were sensitive, intelligent and articulate children, confident and competent in their mother tongue but understandably disadvantaged in English, who needed help with vocabulary and expression in English and not tuition on phonic-based reading schemes. Their own language abilities were being ignored and a chance to explore the creative aspects of English denied them.

5. A proportion of the pupils withdrawn found the experience quite harrowing. They had their confidence destroyed, were labelled by other members of school, and made little progress; they experienced as much difficulty in the mainstream of school as ever.

6. Another adverse aspect of the extensive withdrawal programme in practice was the undesirable attitudes evident in some of the pupils not withdrawn. One class was shown to have an imbalance of abilities, a very large number being deemed 'remedial' and withdrawn from some lessons, leaving a small number of more able pupils who began to exhibit elitist viewpoints. This obviously undermined the school's commitment to mixed-ability teaching.

7. Lastly, pupils withdrawn were doing work largely unrelated to the general curriculum of the school. The work was irrelevant to most aspects of the pupils' needs and lives and individual requirements were not really catered for.

In response to anxieties such as these, an Educational Support and Development Department was established in 1983. We felt that our priority should be to assess accurately the needs of the large numbers of students who were being withdrawn for reading lessons. Did they really need the kind of support they were getting? One new member of the department decided to abandon the standardized reading tests and develop an assessment related to the reading skills needed in class or in their daily life. The new assessment system comprised (a) silent reading, comprehension, prediction; (b) miscue analysis, reading aloud, comprehension, prediction; (c) cloze procedure,

125

prediction; and (d) an informal chat about reading and learning at five different levels to cover the ranges of ability of the pupils being assessed. A check list was designed to record such things as the difficulties pupils experienced and attitudes they displayed to reading. Although the number of pupils who would need reading support was expected to be quite high, it was discovered very few pupils actually needed much support.

Once assessments were complete, the redefining of the Department's role began in earnest. As a Department we had two major aims which determined our way forward. Firstly, to promote the benefits of mixed-ability teaching by showing in principle our firm opposition to withdrawal of pupils from lessons, which tends to undermine the purpose of mixed-ability teaching. Secondly, to establish curriculum-wide, in-class support with a view to assessing its practice. The purpose of this self-assessment was to bring attention to the underlying philosophy of what we were trying to do and develop work more systematically across the curriculum. We were helped in this by the Language and Learning Committee.

This group gave us an ideal forum for explaining changes we were making and an opportunity to encounter other people's ideas on collaborative teaching and collaborative learning. Ideally, we wanted our insights into the learning process to be incorporated at all levels, to be involved in developments in as many subjects as possible. To this end, discussion in the Language and Learning Committee was invaluable. We were able to create dialogues about such issues as the extent to which the language skills of pupils with varying special needs were being addressed in the classroom. We could discuss the way tasks set allowed for enjoyment and involvement in reading. We could examine together the extent to which students were being presented either with over-simplified work sheets that demanded no serious reading or with too difficult work sheets, sometimes written out in almost illegible handwriting.

The Committee proved invaluable to us in giving us regular and systematic feedback on what was happening in the departments and enabled us to build on contacts with teachers who, right from the outset, were amenable to the idea of having a support teacher in their classrooms and willing to engage in collaborative teaching.

When pupils were first placed back into mainstream classes, it was essential for us to monitor their progress and see how well they could cope. Our observations revealed interesting results which we reported on at the Language and Learning Committee meetings. We found a lot of pupils had their time wasted by having to listen (without properly understanding) to a lot of formal instruction. There was not sufficient opportunity provided in classrooms for collaborative work and group talk. Besides talk being the focus of a task itself, for developing social and oral skills, pupils were often not able to talk enough to come to terms with difficult ideas. In some classrooms, planned work was not always accessible to all pupils. There appeared to be either not enough stimulation or not enough 'ground work' being done. Lastly, we observed an extensive preoccupation with writing but there generally did not appear to be enough variety between types of writing pupils were being asked to do. Much time, particularly for the less able, was spent copying or occupied with passive writing exercises which were not developing their critical reading or writing skills. We saw the need to begin the long process of helping create suitable conditions to allow pupils to begin controlling their own learning more.

Part of our effort to help create suitable conditions for learning did involve some small group withdrawal, despite that being contrary to our philosophy. However, because of the failure in some lessons to provide opportunities for genuine collaborative learning we still had withdrawal groups for a very small number of pupils in order to offer more constructive conditions than could be provided in sometimes over-formal and traditional classes. This withdrawal system operated for only first and second years and we felt it should be flexible enough to encompass all kinds of special needs and to allow movement between mainstream and small groups. We considered the withdrawal groups to be an effective teaching context because of the opportunity for pupils to get individual help specifically geared towards their needs. The withdrawal group was used for the extension of, or preparation for, mainstream work. We were very pleased to notice that increasingly subject teachers began approaching teachers of small groups asking that homework be discussed and general pre-teaching and back-up material be worked on. This made the small-group lesson much more relevant for the pupils and connected the provision of special help to the main curriculum.

In setting up the classroom support work we felt there were basic important considerations to be kept in mind.

Firstly, we thought quite carefully about who we were going to work with. We initially put out a request sheet for interested staff to complete. We thought carefully about who should work together and aimed at collaborating with people whom we knew well or whose wavelength we shared. It was difficult to meet the requirements of all requests for support teachers, but we positioned ourselves in mixed-ability classes (with the exception of maths and CSE history) as much across the curriculum as possible. The way in which support teachers worked with mainstream teachers varied. It ranged from simply adapting and modifying teaching materials to experimenting with classroom management and organization.

Another important consideration was that the collaboration, at whatever depth, was to develop the skills of the pupils and there should be no pressure or feeling of assessing each partner's abilities as a teacher or attempts to force someone to adopt an attitude they didn't want. Learning together by sharing and example was fine but the ESD Department did not want to impose beliefs on those not open to them.

It was important also to have long-term, regular commitments to collaborations and see the learning of the pupils in its whole context. Alongside this was a belief in a mutual sharing of responsibilities. As real partners in the classroom, support teachers should work equally on management and organization, lesson preparation, marking, devising of assessments, reviewing of materials and school reports. The unwritten rule of sharing tasks equally helps to make sure a potentially awkward relationship is built upon trust and gets off to a good start. We entered into joint policy discussions with various departments, trying to take into account the presence of pupils with special needs and minimize the distinction between 'learning language' and 'learning the subject'. The aim was to ensure all pupils derived maximum benefit from their experience of subject teaching. The joint discussions focused on several proposals:

1.   To get away from the provision of special materials for 'low achievers' in the classes.
2.   To set up ways of organizing group work and oral work around shared tasks to promote language learning.
3.   To provide models of writing and give close support to those pupils not fluent in writing.
4.   To develop methods of assessment and monitoring of pupils' progress in learning.
5.   To look at teaching materials and analyse them for language demands made on pupils.
6.   To work collaboratively on new materials which took all pupils' needs into account.

As partners in the classroom it was less easy to define our roles. In practice, we had two. That of 'specialist' and that of equal partner. As specialists we were language teachers, teaching language in context when and where pupils needed it to communicate. We were trying to bridge the gap between language demands of subjects and the pupils' own language, to raise the status and develop the confidence of pupils with special needs.

At the end of our first full year as a special needs department, we decided to survey the staff by way of a questionnaire to get written feedback on where they felt our strengths and weaknesses lay in order that we could further improve our practice, and to gather information on what mainstream teachers saw as being the prime considerations in a partnership.

The most important factor in the partnership according to most staff was detailed discussions about support work and collaborative teaching to ensure roles are defined and strategies discussed before the work begins. This was closely followed by the feeling that support teachers should have equal status to a mainstream teacher in a classroom. Of obvious importance to all was the necessity for teachers in a partnership to meet before the lesson to discuss materials, strategies and teacher roles. Staff felt failure to do this would result in the work not succeeding.

The next important factor was evaluation of work after a lesson. This, mainly because of time constraints, had not been adequately done but it was felt that, if collaboratively planned materials were to become an integral part of a department's resources, it would be vitally needed. Most people thought regular departmental workshops to plan work, disseminate ideas, and discuss materials were important. The last essential point for consideration in a partnership, was, according to most staff, that the support teacher should work with all pupils in a class. There should be no risk of polarization of groups, or labelling. The collaborative teaching model would encourage collaborative learning and hopefully result in true mixed ability groupings.

It was thought important that adequate time be given to teachers for liaising, for discussion and negotiation of difficulties and so on. It was also felt that even more time is needed for preparation and planning of materials for exam classes. Workshops were, in general, not set up and this made discussion of materials more difficult. The clear need for negotiation and compromise arose in this bracket too. Some people felt that in practice overcoming such difficulties as personality differences and conflict of opinions was evident. However, everyone felt their style of teaching had changed since working collaboratively and all comments made on the questionnaire reflected more thoughtful teachers, more aware of the language needs of their pupils and more thorough and 'inventive' in their approach. All felt they had succeeded in motivating their pupils more, engaging them as active learners, not passive 'listeners' or 'copiers'.

Group work and shared oral tasks were amongst strategies most extensively extended in the new 'cooperative classrooms' and an obvious benefit mentioned was teacher-time with individuals. All pupils had access to two teachers as advisers, consultants, collaborators and negotiators.

Mainstream teachers' reactions to having another teacher working with them in the classroom before the partnerships started and then at the end of a year changed pleasingly. People ranged from feeling

hesitant, defensive, self-conscious and fearful of having lazy methodology exposed to becoming positive about their work and relaxed and
secure about a teacher-partner in their room. Most significantly
people felt a strong commitment to the continuation of collaborative
work and team teaching. They felt more aware of the needs of the
pupils in their classes and as one teacher put it:

> 'I believe now I have greater confidence with regard to the pupils
> with special needs as a result of being able to recognize them as
> being merely at a point on a scale of language development which
> is flexible and in many cases can be quickly improved.'

The ESD Department was delighted with the results of its first four
terms' work when the questionnaires were returned. We felt that in a
very short time we had set up a pattern of cooperative teaching that
had caused a great number of teachers to rethink their role as
teachers and understand a great deal more about their pupils'
learning. No-one wanted to return to a system of wholesale
withdrawal of pupils with special needs from the classroom, and
everyone saw only positive ways forward emerging from the work. In
conclusion, people felt that support departments should begin a
restructuring of their approach slowly if working with teachers new to
the ideas; that support work should range fairly across the age-range;
and that, in the collaborative teaching situation, partners should be
more critical of each others' practice.

Teachers do not find collaborative work easy. It is more demand-
ing, there is never adequate time for discussion and preparation of
materials and there is the question of the 'chemistry' of the teachers
working together. However, through good teacher communications
via such bodies as language and learning committees, discussion can
be established which leads to sound negotiations, trial and error in
practice, and trust.

Chapter 15

Priorities and constraints

John Hickman and Keith Kimberley

We referred at the end of Chapter 11 to the decision to re-establish regular meetings of the full Language and Learning Committee and more explicit sharing of perspectives. The term beginning September 1984 provided a lull in the industrial action being taken and an opportunity for a return to an earlier pattern of working. As the school was in the middle of planning a Community Week in which all the local community agencies were involved, Barbara Holden, the Outreach Teacher, was asked to talk to the Committee about her work and what was involved, for her, in the moves to make Forest Gate a Community School. This, together with the Community Week itself in the following month, put the relation of the school to the people who live in Forest Gate firmly in our minds when we came to plan succeeding activities.

The following meeting decided that we should take on a study of the Report of the Inner London Education Authority's (ILEA) Hargreaves Committee which had just completed a review of the secondary curriculum in the ILEA. Jon McGill offered to present a brief digest for the Committee on *Improving Secondary Schools*, as the Report was called. It was stated that, as new activities were beginning, the Committee again should advertise itself as an open forum and every encouragement given to other members of staff to attend.

One consequence of this openness was an offer from the Craft, Design, and Technology Department to do a presentation of the kind described in Chapter 3 about work in their subject. As members of this Department had not sent a representative, and had always been somewhat sceptical about its value, this was an offer that we gratefully accepted. The proposed work on the Hargreaves' Report also drew in the Head Teacher Mrs Anne Rowland, to the Committee's meetings.

The brief of the ILEA Committee had been to:

consider the curriculum and organization of ILEA secondary
schools as they affect pupils mainly in the age range 11-16 but also
those remaining in the sixth form for one year.

with special attention to be given to issues of underachievement and
nonattendance and it was very clear to the Head, as to us that the
Report had touched on matters of significance for secondary schools
in other LEAs. Not for the first time, the Language and Learning
Committee was taking on board wider perspectives and, on this
occasion, the Head was keen to take part in systematic discussions
about the future of secondary schools in the inner cities, which she
felt warranted her presence and full involvement.

Jon McGill's presentation highlighted the ways in which the
Report analysed achievement, and defined the social contexts in
which the ILEA schools are situated. He also drew attention to the
Report's analysis of teacher attitudes and expectations. He endorsed
nearly all the recommendations, though he did suggest that they
would remain merely 'interesting research and speculation' if
'unnourished for lack of funds' and expressed some scepticism about
the level of interest in the Hargreaves' Report likely to be expressed
in Newham.

As a result of this first meeting, the issues raised by the Report
were divided up into sixteen sections and members of the Language
and Learning Committee made offers to present the ideas in the
Report, together with an analysis of their strengths and weaknesses
and implications for Forest Gate School (see appendix
Document 3). A timetable from January to September was organized, with nineteen people signing up for a half session. This meant
that no-one had more than eight or nine pages to read and would
have plenty of time to think about the issues in relation to the
School's own practice.

In the event (and most unfortunately given the level of commitment to the enterprise), only the first meeting was held since, by the
date for the second meeting, we were deeply involved in the long,
bruising, period of industrial action which was to stretch from
January 1985 to May 1986. There is little that can be said in the book
about this period for, in terms of the kind of work that has been
described so far, everything came to a halt and we entered a period
marked by the decline in our morale as teachers. It is difficult to see
yourself as part of a valued profession, working to improve the
quality of children's learning, when embattled with a government
which is determined to suppress teachers' pay; unilaterally alter
teachers' conditions of service; and recast the whole education system
to different ends than those espoused by most inner-city LEAs. As
we noted in relation to the first period of industrial action, teachers

who decide to 'withdraw goodwill' do this in full cognizance of the effect of this on their own effectiveness in the classroom and on their students. We were very conscious that our optimism about our work and those elements of our jobs which make them challenging and enjoyable were, in this period, severely constrained by the circumstances we found ourselves in.

Thus, it was not until July 1986 that we met again as a Language and Learning Committee. This meeting was to review past work and an opportunity to plan an agenda for the school year 1986-7. John Hickman wrote to all teaching staff:

> During the past six years the school's Language and Learning Committee has met fairly regularly, although industrial action has seemingly occurred even more regularly.
>
> It is an open committee and almost all curriculum areas are represented. In the past we have shared departmental philosophies and practices; read some books on theory together and engaged in school-based research. We were about to embark upon a study of the Hargreaves' Report when the most recent phase of industrial action began.
>
> I'm going to reconvene the committee on Monday, 7 July at 3.50 p.m. in A9 and you'd be very welcome either to observe or participate. Attendance doesn't imply commitment.

The invitation resulted in a meeting at which a series of suggestions were discussed which ranged from an idea for a review of the school's language and learning needs leading to explicit, written policy to a plea for people to spend time observing each other's lessons to help increase sensitivity and improve teaching. Transition from primary to secondary school was thought worth studying, as were ideas on purposeful reading; girls in science; and bilingualism. Interest in small-scale research was not in the foreground but neither had it disappeared completely from the agenda.

In September 1986, however, none of these proposals from the July meeting was strong enough, as the fourth year began its new syllabuses, to take precedence over preoccupation with the General Certificate of Secondary Education (GCSE). We can now see that work connected with the new examination did not have the same radical quality that the still-born sessions on the Hargreaves' Report had promised. It was, we still think, important for ideas about the new examination to be shared across departments and for the teachers to take the time to rethink, and make explicit to others, the nature of the changes involved. However, we do not think that, in those circumstances, there was any real likelihood of discussion moving on to fundamental questions about learning. By the end of the term, the programme of presentations had, for many, become an unwanted chore. Reading through the minutes of the GCSE meetings on English, maths, religious studies, CDT, we are struck by the useful insights into the potential of open-ended questions and course-work. We also note that the Committee discussed ways in which the new syllabuses, by giving more responsibility to the teachers, might provide answers to the criticisms of previous syllabuses raised by the Race and Gender research group. Srima Perera also outlined to one of these meetings a plan for monitoring the attitude and progress through the fourth and fifth year of four girls who had been good at science in their third year. But, in spite of the positive moments, we have to acknowledge that the sessions had become lifeless and, when the humanities and science session had to be abandoned because of poor attendance, John Hickman, as before in the group's history, wrote an open letter suggesting that if the Committee was to retain any credibility the programme would have to be radically changed.

The reshaping that followed was based on a review of in-service provision (INSET) in the School. Under new arrangements for funding in-service initiatives LEAs are obliged to make bids for government money and have to specify well in advance those intentions that do not coincide with government priorities. This means that schools, in turn, now have to identify, plan, and cost their in-service needs through the Grant Related In-Service Training (GRIST) arrangements, to be handed on to the LEA coordinator, and John Hickman, as a senior teacher, had been given responsibility for coordinating these arrangements in the School.

Perhaps because of this, and the overlap between much of the work of the Language and Learning Committee and INSET, the Committee discussed the new arrangements at length. This discussion, it now appears, pre-figured the winding up of the Language and Learning Committee but some important future activities were planned which drew on the classroom research 'tradition' of the Committee rather than being instigated by the new GRIST arrangements. For example, Bernice Adkins, Keith Mears, Naz Rassool and Rosemary Lucas had formed a working party to focus on the needs of bilingual students and Srima Perera (her first investigation having collapsed for reasons beyond her control) had devised a question-naire by which she was to look at the perceptions of science by boys and girls in the first and second years. A further idea which emerged from this meeting was for the Committee to set itself the 'achievable goal' of sharing ideas on marking.

All three of these initiatives were later reported back to the Committee. The responses to Srima Perera's survey indicated that, as far as could be ascertained, boys and girls in the first and second years saw themselves as equally proficient in science and future investigations were planned with respect to option choices in the third year. The planned work on marking generated a long and interesting discussion on why we mark; departmental representatives describing their ways of responding to written work; and considering the nature of student-teacher discussions about progress. There was felt to be a need for some sort of school statement about drafting and marking which could be communicated to parents. These meetings also included reports from the school's Primary Liaison Committee and were attended by representatives from two of our feeder primary schools. The work of the Bilingualism Working Party is discussed more fully later in this chapter.

Nevertheless in the changed climate of 1987, and with a contract being imposed on the teaching profession, voluntary activities like participation in the Language and Learning Committee had become a luxury. John Hickman sent out a letter gently bringing its operations to a close (see Appendix Document 5). It reflected the changed circumstances of teachers and brought to an end six years of varied activities. Remarking on the successful history of the group, John Hickman suggested that members of the Language and Learning Committee might wish to join a Staff Development Committee which was being set up as a forum for INSET ideas, initiatives, and planning. This Committee, like its Language and Learning pre-decessor, has cross-curriculum representation and its twice-termly meetings (in Directed Time) are open to the whole teaching staff. Its functions are to:

1. Represent the views of all the staff on INSET priorities.
2. Help plan a coherent School policy for INSET which caters for as wide a range of needs as possible.
3. Ensure fairness in the distribuition of GRIST funds.
4. Monitor any GRIST initiative.
5. Ensure proper feedback from any courses attended.
6. Help organize staff meetings where the yearly Institutional Development Plan (IDP) is discussed and formulated.
7. Review all aspects of the GRIST scheme.

Unlike the Language and Learning Committee, its brief is specific, with the mechanisms for the operation of its functions and the relationship of coordinator, committee, and staff meeting laid down explicitly. (There is, for example, no choice about helping to organize staff meetings to discuss the IDP or ensuring proper feedback from people who have benefited from INSET.) At the time of writing the Staff Development Committee is deciding on priorities for INSET in 1988/9.

A possible way in which the legacy of the Language and Learning Committee may continue to influence school-based INSET can be seen in the work of the Bilingualism Working Party briefly referred to above. This group followed a pattern set by sub-groups of the Language and Learning Committee and, in particular, there is continuity of concern with the work on ESL provision which was reported in Chapter 11. A report from the Bilingualism Working Party to the Language and Learning Committee in March 1986 made this particularly clear. General discussion centred round what mainstream teachers need to know, and do, in order to meet the needs of students with little, or no, English. Ways of making classroom activities work for all students were explored through a workshop approach which generated questions about the consequences of setting separate material for second language learners. A teacher from one of the local primary schools was able to report on the way in which support could be offered in a primary classroom. Members of the Working Party were made aware of the difficulties children suffer in transferring from the security of a single base to the subject-dominated secondary school. It seemed a high priority for the group to find ways of easing transfer, especially for students needing ESL support. Some of the ideas to be pursued were: to make speedy and reliable assessment of levels of literacy and to gather sufficient information on home languages and levels of proficiency in them to enable the support teachers to respond to each student's needs appropriately. The environment of the school itself needed to be more welcoming to bilingual students, with notices and letters available in a number of languages. The workshop activity which was tried out here was later to provide the basis for a full-scale session for the whole staff and the support departments proceeded to implement some of the suggestions relating to transfer.

It is significant that this group did not approach the staff as a whole with the diffidence that had plagued earlier groups and it may be worth spelling out why we think this was the case. Firstly, they were not operating in a vacuum but building on previous work. This was of two kinds: the general acknowledgement of welcoming of diversity, marked by the Forest Gate Language Survey (see appendix, Document 4) used as part of the First-Year English curriculum from 1982 and the inclusion of Urdu and Panjabi in the fourth- and fifth-year choices as part of the Modern Languages offered; and the work done on changing ESL provision by changing its structure. Secondly, the Working Party was not having to decide whether or not it had something useful to report from its research but was proposing that wider discussion was needed and that, to this end, it would be necessary to bring in outsiders. This was part of the third factor which shows in the shift in terminology; in the move from considering the needs of the ESL and mainstream teachers to a consideration of the needs of the bilingual student. This change in perspective meant that, in proposing INSET sessions for everyone, speakers would be needed who could not only give up-to-date thinking on how to support young people who have the potential to grow up bilingual, or multilingual, but also people who could describe the issues from the point of view of the bilingual language user. It was a shift in ideology which meant looking to the community for speakers and putting in the centre of the picture the experience of the bilingual student.

The Working Party was keen that the staff of Forest Gate should be aware of the implications of this ideological shift and recognize the strength of the argument that schools should support the develop-ment of a full range of language skills in all its students, developing, where appropriate, their skills and awareness as bilinguals and not merely emphasizing the learning of English. In an MA dissertation, written at this time, Naz Rassool one of the Working Party, made this point even more strongly:

> Policy needs to define the social groups for which it caters as well as the purpose of bilingualism for the speakers. Emphasis purely on providing for the linguistic diversity within society provides an inadequate rationale for bilingualism.

and that

> for real change to be effected, policy needs to challenge the predominantly mono-cultural and mono-linguistic perspective.
>
> (Rassool, 1986)

She argued that a comprehensive language policy for the education of all students could not simply content itself with language learning but had to be combined with the development of a critical social awareness which is able to lay bare:

> the power relations in a fundamentally unequal society.

These important changes in perception crucially influenced the five INSET sessions that were arranged for the summer term, using GRIST funding. The first session concentrated on the students' experience and used workshop strategies thought out by Bernice Adkins and Keith Mears and already tried out on the Language and Learning Committee. Tasks were given to groups who then reported back with the result that the next day the entire wall outside the staff room was covered in ideas from the groups. The following session was given by representatives of five of the school's main linguistic (and in some cases religious) communities, who gave their views on the situation their children find themselves in and the ways in which they can be helped. Only then in the sequence was there a session on second language learning and this of an unexpected kind. Staff found that they were cast in the role of students in a mainstream home

137

economics lesson, conducted first in Spanish and subsequently in French. The two remaining sessions were used for brainstorming for positive ways of assisting complete beginners and a session on reinforcing and using the students' linguistic knowledge and awareness. Reasonably content that the issues they had first met to discuss were now being addressed by many more people, the Working Party disbanded.

It was agreed that there should be a series of practical consequences stemming from the INSET work described above. New students, who need support in their learning of English, could be given two students to take care of them, and tutor groups helped to understand what it is like to arrive on your own in a new school. Volunteers are being sought from outside the school to help with translation and act as interpreters when needed. However, the session in which representatives from the communities spoke may ultimately have the most lasting effects. (Summaries of their contributions are included as Document 6 in the Appendix.) For example, in response to the expression of surprise from some of the staff that more emphasis had not been placed by the speakers on the importance of their children learning English effectively it was pointed out:

1. This is an area of concern for parents but that other concerns are of equal, if not paramount, importance.
2. The learning of English is not separable from the general learning environment created by the school and society. If, effectively, these are inhospitable environments for members of the communities, the learning of English will not be effective.
3. Support for the mother tongue remains a crucial issue: it enhances, rather than detracts from, the linguistic development of the bilingual learner in English as it gives status to the student's existing language competence.

This challenge to the school to go further than its use of one peripatetic, mother-tongue teacher who teaches small groups of fourth- and fifth-year students, was echoed by Mike Mobbs from the Newham South Asian Languages Team when he outlined current provision in the Borough, which is geared to examination forms in secondary schools and restricted to three languages: Hindi, Urdu, and Panjabi. He argued that proper support for mother-tongue development would require teaching to be available at a much earlier stage in students' education. By the fourth year, students have already, in many cases, lost ground in mother tongue literacy, have therefore lost motivation and see their mother tongue as given secondary status in comparison with other subjects on offer. This reflects the status schools give to the home languages of its students.

138

He advocated that Forest Gate School needed to consider the raising of the profile of languages other than English in the school generally, not only through being sensitive at the level of signs, notices, letters to parents, handbooks, reception procedures and so on but also by the inclusion of other languages in the modern languages repertoire throughout the school and by teaching some mainstream subjects through the medium of the mother tongue. The difficulties involved in making changes of this order are, of course, considerable but we take note of the challenge offered and of the extent to which we are now willing to think about issues which earlier were not even in our consciousness. As we write, a teacher of Bengali is being sought to teach in the fourth and fifth years in response to the changing linguistic profile of the school and an evening class, aimed primarily at teachers, Bangla for beginners, has just begun.

Part Four
Teachers Learning

Chapter 16

Language and learning: policy and process

John Hickman and Keith Kimberley

One question that has haunted us since we undertook this writing up has been whether focusing on language and learning is not merely unfashionable (who boasts of their Bullock Language Policy now-adays?) but also misguided. We remain unrepentant.

Noble as the sentiments in the policies drawn up in the wake of the Bullock Report were, they often remained statements of principle and assertions of theory. They rarely described a process of learning being undertaken by the teachers involved and they had little vision of the possibility that they might need to be responsive to changing contexts. All too often the policy consisted of a document written to meet the demand from the LEA – and no more.

We chose to emphasize process. Put that bluntly, it sounds sterile but we think it is not in practice, because what we mean by process in relation to language policy is the establishing of priorities which are open to change as the context changes; realized in a programme of activities leading to some dead ends and some new horizons. With all its faults, we think the Language and Learning Committee has been a mechanism for achieving such ends; keeping a close relationship between ideas and practice. Instead of a policy document, we have a variety of documents, reflecting different stages in people's thinking, and marking out changes in priorities. Some of these were intended to be ephemeral, others (such as the ones included in this book) written with wider audiences in mind. Instead of a set of language guidelines, we have a changing agenda, responsive to changes taken place in, and outside, the school. The varied activities we have engaged in have become the history of this continuously developing policy.

A second question that we have had to face has been raised by others, as well as within the Committee, and concerns the limits which should be set for our activities. One consequence of accepting a changing agenda is that, at times, groups will want to stretch their original terms of reference to their limits. We were no exception. These pressures for exploring wider and wider issues both seem desirable and sound out dangers for the credibility of a group which has been given a specific brief. However, we suggest that it is necessary to bear in mind that a committee whose terms of reference are language and learning does not fit comfortably into any school category; inevitably the whole range of what is taught, and how it is taught, comes into the compass of the Committee. As a result, the central question about the effectiveness of children's learning, which is so threatening to many of us, often generates the complaint that a language and learning committee is out of order in asking it.

We also think that it would be very foolish to deny the value of pursuing wider social and political issues which members of a group think are relevant to the classroom. The Language and Learning Committee would have been greatly impoverished if these wider perspectives had not informed people's thinking, though we acknowledge that such discussion is often contentious and difficult. Neither would it seem reasonable to deny to such a group the possibility of exploring issues which will require to be implemented as school policy. If this had been the case there would not have been the opportunity for ideas on ESL provision, for example, to be tried out before implementation. We do not, however, wish to argue that a committee of this kind should go off in any direction which takes someone's fancy – even that of the Senior Teacher with responsibility for Language Across the Curriculum!

The way that the Forest Gate Language and Learning Committee changed its course at various times suggests that this is unlikely to happen. We notice that, at key moments, lengthy discussions ensued about the way forward. This willingness to accommodate ideas coming from people with different preoccupations and disciplinary backgrounds seems to have ensured that the priorities we finally chose had broad and principled support. Thus, across its history, the Committee established a multidimensional language agenda which encompassed a wide range of interrelated elements, within a broad framework where it was possible to pose questions about language, and languages, in society. It is thus appropriate that questions of race, gender, and class have occupied positions in the foreground of our discussions and, similarly, that the role of community languages, and the purposes for which the students may wish to use them, has had more prominence than it might have received some years ago.

The Committee has centrally been concerned with children's development as language users and their encounters with a school's curriculum. We have investigated aspects of talking, writing, and reading in relation to students' learning, with the emphasis sometimes on one of these and sometimes on another. In our history, almost against wider trends, talk has had more attention than reading (the preoccupation of the nation in the 1970s) and writing (its preoccupation in the 1980s).

A third question that we have reflected on is whether, despite attempts to frame it differently, the Language and Learning Committee ended up by being dominated by the English Department, or by its Head of Department who chaired the Committee. We must here acknowledge that our view is partial and that, though our answer is a guarded negative, we recognize both that members of the English Department, along with key others, have played a very important role in breathing life into its projects and also that John Hickman has played a decisive part in maintaining its continuity and its characteristic informal style.

Some of the attempts to get language across the curriculum policies going in the 1970s were stopped in their tracks after a few months, or even weeks, either by the over-zealous role taken by English teachers or by the use of top-down models of innovation. The problem was neatly summarized by HMI in *Bullock Revisited* (DES, 1985).

> The very phrase 'Language Across the Curriculum' can suggest something imposed from above upon the various subject departments of a school. The idea of a policy embodied in the organisational structure of the school, desirable as it is, may have been seen by some teachers as a requirement to adapt themselves to a theory derived from a subject discipline other than their own.

By contrast with the Bullock phraseology, HMI suggest that it is difficult for any teacher to reject the ideas involved if they are presented in terms of learning.

> A teacher of science or geography, for example, whose concern is simply to impart facts to his pupils, who checks their absorption of these only by questions demanding short factual answers, who dictates quantities of notes without considering whether the vocabulary and structures he uses are intelligible to his pupils, who devises worksheets that take no account of his pupils' language competence – the problem with such a teacher is that he is using limited and ineffective methods of teaching science or geography. Good teachers of these and other subjects know that pupils learn and understand better if they are able to ask questions, to explore and discuss the matters presented to them, to sift and relate evidence, to speculate, to work towards conclusions, to bring ideas into full understanding by expressing them in their own words,

143

while learning progressively how to express them in ways appropriate to the discipline of the subject.

We have been fortunate to find ourselves among teachers who, whatever their subject, have been interested in how they can teach their subjects better and we would like to think that the ways of working of the Language and Learning Committee have been in the spirit of the second, rather than the first, quotation (though there may be those who know us well who would disagree). The early work of the Committee demonstrates, we think, that the starting points of subject teachers, other than English, were regarded as the appropriate places to begin studies of learning. We do not think that a voluntary group of teachers is likely to go on meeting if they see little benefit to themselves or the school or if they feel that their contributions are not being valued and given space. People will not maintain an interest if they think that the ideas generated by the group working together are seen as the property of one individual. A group of this kind (like this book) is as strong as the combination of voices that speaks out from it.

More specifically, the role that John Hickman has had with relation to the Committee, as Senior Teacher with responsibility for Language Across the Curriculum (impossible as it is for the coauthors to analyse this objectively) has generated both advantages and disadvantages for the group. However democratic the style of a committee of this kind may be, it is not possible to ignore that whoever coordinates, minutes, and chairs the committee will impose on its workings some of their own preoccupations, concerns, and personality. It is also important to remember that the 'Senior Teacher' designation carries with it the responsibility to make things happen. Both these factors have an influence on staff opinion of a language and learning enterprise. However much bridge-building is attempted, and however much a committee is in the hands of its members, there is no guarantee that the 'Englishness' of the project won't aggravate some people and that the role of language and learning coordinator be subject to some adverse criticism.

In the end we think (again subjectively) that the Language and Learning Committee's longevity and achievements result from two main factors:

1. Success in making reciprocal relationships through cross-department contact in which there was substantial agreement that expertise concerning language was not confined to a few specialist teachers, and
2. A widely shared belief that expertise about language and learning could be developed by teachers themselves undertaking

investigations; planning their own programmes of reading; and establishing networks of contact with others.

These do not account for the importance of accident in the history of schools and the way in which some groups are more able than others to establish common ground and enjoy working together but they do account, we think, for the amount of serious, sustained activity that was engaged in and of which this book records a part.

As we were coming to the end of the process of writing down the history of the Language and Learning Committee, we asked current members of the Committee, a few past members, and Mrs Anne Rowland, Head Teacher, to write down some reflections on the phenomena with which they had been involved and, in particular, to analyse its strengths and weaknesses. One of the responses, from Jon McGill, took the form of a letter, written in the cogent, combative style to which we have become accustomed. Because he pinpoints our own main dilemmas in analysing the wide range of activities with which we have been concerned across several years, we have included it almost in full.

The great value of a committee such as the one formed at Forest Gate was chiefly intellectual. The practical necessities of school work and the demands of subject teaching have a tendency to isolate individuals, both in subject area terms and in terms of sharing experiences. Teachers in secondary schools often have only one obvious, common experience, that of being involved in the learning process. However, my experience teaches me that we stop examining that process and our roles in it very early on in our careers. Therefore, membership of a committee which is designated as investigative of language and learning experience proved useful.

Among the uses:
  (a) identifying common objectives;
  (b) relating different experiences in an effort to better understand work done outside our own subject area or responsibility;
  (c) the Committee, with representation across the school, forced a unity upon us which might not otherwise have existed;
  (d) it provided a stimulus to examine old practice, look into 'esoteric' topics, justify to colleagues practices they might want either to question or to become aware of;
  (d) the Committee gave a respectability to 'academic' pursuits by staff. One of the great ironies of teaching is that, very often, teachers treat their colleagues who have an

145

'academic' bent in similar ways to those shown by youngsters who tease 'brainy' class-mates. Somehow we carry into adulthood a conflicting view of the 'intellectual'. Indeed, commonplace views of teachers as a group tend to the 'anti-intellectual', a distrust of their own *raison d'être*.

The 'problems' encountered: one obvious problem is how to relate the committee and what it does to those staff who take no part. We did not solve this problem – indeed it remained a dilemma for us. We did not wish to foment the anti-intellectual response by being too public, too forceful, yet some of our conclusions about the work of the school demanded widespread attention and action. This dilemma was made more intense by the schizophrenic approach of the management of the school which was, in my view, another by-product of intellectual distrust. Clearly, those responsible for good schools encourage initiatives from within the staff. In-school INSET can be very rewarding and, equally, be prestigious for the school and the reputation of its managers. Equally, the kind of critical research which committees like the Language and Learning group undertake can be expected to highlight weaknesses in school organization and philosophy. This creates an ambivalent attitude – is the committee a lap dog or a serious attempt at active research? I felt we experienced this uncertainty in our work on the 'Multicultural' Working Party. The school required a symbol of commitment but perhaps staff felt less committed to the substance.

Areas of the Committee's work which were most valuable? Just meeting together was of value – but the specific items, for me, were those where staff presented topics. These presentations were of use to the presenter as much as those in the 'audience'. I feel that our Committee forces people out of an 'anti-intellectualism' which proposes that research is for others. The problem with such a line of approach is that it allows others to dictate to us what our own experiences mean.

We share with Jon McGill the view that the central function of teachers is to concern themselves with students' learning and that it is this fact which should provide commitment by all teachers to exploring the relationship of language and learning. We also find plausible his explanation that the difficulty in making such an operation a success lies partly in the anti-intellectual stance adopted by many in the teaching profession. We believe, as strongly as we did in 1981, that understanding how students learn, and what gets in the way of their learning, should interest all teachers but we know that the Committee did not succeed in convincing everyone, even in one school, that this warrants people meeting together for such activities as: explaining to each other their ways of teaching; examining textbooks; listening to tapes of classroom interaction and so on. Moreover, we are particularly conscious that a group which engages in such activities will always run the risk of being perceived as elitist, especially if they touch on contentious issues such as race, class, and gender or begin to suggest that changes may be necessary in whole-school policy. Ironically, the more confident those participating become (to the point of writing up presentations; giving talks to outside groups; conducting surveys; and trying out techniques of participant observation in each others' classrooms) the more likely it is that they will be perceived as a group apart, uninterested in other views than their own.

The letter also points to the difficult and contradictory position of the Committee in the School's structure. Anyone who has borne with us this far will be aware that the Committee was set up to be representative of all departments – but voluntary; it was to consider aspects of teaching and learning central to the curriculum and organization of the school but had no policy-making role. We think these contradictions help to explain why the position of the Committee in the life of the school, and in its relation to the management structure, has been, by turns, productive and proble-matic. It has, for example, taken on such varied patterns of activity that keeping track of them, and their possible consequences, has been difficult for those not closely involved. It has, at times, pursued its own directions, as with its research programme, while, at others, it has been responsive to school-wide concerns, as with the Bilingualism Working Party. Sometimes it has been at the centre of a major school initiative, as with the development of the support departments, and occasionally has gone off into the stratosphere, as with some of the reading for seminars. What we would describe as flexibility has been seen by others as an irritating tendency to want a finger in every pie.

We have some reservations about Jon McGill's assessment of the relationship between the Committee and the school's management team. In our perspective, we would want to acknowledge the importance of the Headteacher's role in the creation of space, and legitimation, for the Committee. It seems to us that this involved a level of risk-taking, especially when the Committee was pushing at the boundaries of the limits she had set for its operations. On the other hand we think he has put his finger on a vital point in describing the uneasy relationship which can exist between those responsible for the outward face of a school and groups of teachers who have been given sufficient autonomy to develop new, and perhaps uncomfort-able initiatives. Just as encouraging critical awareness in the students we teach can involve us in discussion of uncomfortable contradic-tions, encouraging teachers to think for themselves can lead to the

147

exposure of the weaknesses in a school as well as its strengths.

It was generally agreed by those we questioned that the difficulties and contradictions we have been outlining created substantial weaknesses in the work of the Committee. We had 'taken on too much'; had made 'insufficient contact with fundamentally different viewpoints held in the school'; and had not always managed to make our work sufficiently well-defined and precise, resorting to 'political polemic' rather than winning hearts and minds. Mrs Anne Rowland, the Headteacher, suggested that the nearer the Committee got to policy issues the more it mattered that it was not rigorously representative of the whole staff. She also commented that the Committee had worked best when tightly chaired, with the corollary that she suspected it worked less well when functioning in sub-groups.

On the other hand, people had, like Jon McGill, many positive things to say. Most reported a broadening of their personal perspectives, a development in confidence in handling ideas, and benefits derived from closely examining their practice. They had valued the focused nature of exchanges of views across subjects, and thought particularly useful both the research which had been undertaken and the presentations by staff who had expertise the others did not possess. The Headteacher also reflected on the positive gains; itemizing the emphasis on pedagogy and mixed-ability methodology; the cross-fertilisation between departments; and the equal opportunities focus.

We find it interesting that, among the benefits to the departments and the school, many of the things we ourselves believe to be central were included. We would not wish to suggest that activities in the Committee dramatically changed departments' ways of working but we, too, would claim that there has been some indirect influence on practice and some erosion of traditional barriers. A commonly held view, with which we also concur, is that the Committee was a good place to try out ideas, such as those which informed the changes in second language teaching and supporting students with special learning difficulties. In this context we think it is worth remarking that it is not always easy to recognize that teachers whom we meet every day in the staff room may be, slowly but surely, establishing new ideas and procedures in their specialist areas. A prophet is often unacknowledged in his, or her, own staff room. Similarly, we think that the changes in knowledge and perspective with respect to racism and sexism which have occurred in the history of the Committee have demanded opportunities for lengthy and far-reaching discussion of the kind which the Committee was established to facilitate. The more difficult and complex issues are, the more time is needed for careful analysis.

We asked people to think about interaction in the Committee and were mildly surprised by the consistent emphasis of their comments. These referred to the benefits generated by general open-mindedness and tolerance of differing views; willingness of others to listen; respect given to individual intellectual interests; and opportunities to think aloud. Informality, enthusiasm, and the maintaining of positive attitudes (particularly in adversity) were listed to the point where we wondered if people were talking about the Committee we knew. Considering more deeply, we wonder if some of these elements may be of great importance. Are these factors the glue that holds together such a diversity of enterprises? How significant was it that the mode of working was collaborative, and the style welcoming and nonhierarchical? We propose that they were vital elements – though perhaps it sounds trite to say so.

When people volunteered in 1981 to join the Language and Learning Committee they had a variety of reasons. Some wanted to overcome the isolation of the subject specialist; some wanted to relate theory to practice; some wanted to work on projects; some to improve their practice; some wanted to initiate change in the curriculum and organization of the school. We have asked ourselves whether the situation in schools is now so different that teachers coming together for a similar enterprise (the language agenda is still insistent) would have different motives. We hope not, just as we hope the Staff Development Committee will copy the best, and learn from the mistakes, of its predecessor.

Chapter 17

Contracts, professional development, and research

John Hickman and Keith Kimberley

When we began gathering together teachers' writing and keeping records of the processes involved when teachers take on responsibility for their own learning, we did not envisage how much our preconceptions would have to be revised nor that, in the timescale we proposed, there would be a long, damaging period of industrial action. We had been encouraged to start writing by Jean Bleach, Director of the Schools' Council Language for Learning Project, and we expected our efforts to fit neatly into what we saw as well-established patterns of school-based curriculum development and action research. In part, we derived these models from earlier teacher collaborative work on language reported in *Language, the Learner and the School* (Barnes et al., 1969), *Understanding Children Talking* (Martin et al., 1976), *Communication and Learning in Small Groups* (Barnes and Todd, 1977), *The Resources of Classroom Language* (Richmond, 1982), and *Becoming Our Own Experts* (Talk Workshop Group, 1982). What we have written has taken us into broader cultural and political frameworks than we expected and we know that the effects of consistent denigration of teachers and attacks on comprehensive education, culminating in the imposition of a contract and the construction of a new Education Act, have dampened, if not destroyed, many teachers' commitment to the improvement of schools.

We were also influenced in our early thinking by past and current research projects, specifically those which made much use of teachers in developing and trialing materials and approaches. The Language for Learning Project, with which the London Association for the Teaching of English (LATE) Talk Working Party had a close association, was itself based on a model which, although it was located in LEAs' INSET arrangements, relied heavily on teachers agreeing to reflect on what was being achieved in their classrooms; and to do this mostly in addition to their normal teaching and INSET sessions attended. We took for granted that teachers would probably

150

Professional development

In the course of working upon this book, we have regularly found ourselves considering the kind of support needed for teachers' professional development. Our starting point is a consideration of the need for the work that teachers do to be more highly regarded for we cannot afford to have a demoralized teaching force, or even one which does what is legally required without enthusiasm. If either were to happen, it will be the students, and particularly those in inner-city schools, who will suffer, however closely specified the national curriculum may be and however many tests are administered to check attainments. This was put very well by a secondary headteacher, Michael Duffy, in response to the Government's programme of reform, arguing that its policy for the curriculum would do little, or nothing, to improve schools,

> What we need, if we are to achieve better schools, is good teachers: teachers with intelligence, expertise, commitment, energy; teachers with a sense of vocation, responsibility, and a sense of esteem; teachers who feel, in the fashionable jargon of management, that they 'own the job'. Without such teachers the best possible curriculum is no more than one lesson after another.
>
> (*The TES*, 18.9.87)

If teachers are to feel the job is worth doing, it is not simply a matter of proper remuneration (though this is always the main, visible evidence of how they are valued). They also need to be able to see themselves as directly responsible for the learning of their students and able to improve the quality of that learning by taking on new ideas and developing new skills. This necessitates some degree of autonomy.

Genuine professional development does not, in our view, take place just because an INSET course is provided or because an 'expert' is invited into a school to perform. INSET is perhaps at its most effective when seen as a response to the identified needs of a school and based on the perceptions of the teachers about their practice. It may be difficult to quantify the outcomes of such school-centred activities but how does one assess a change of attitude, or an increased awareness or a subtle development of understanding? How does one measure the effects that grow from the seed of an idea, which is lodged in someone's mind in the autumn term but is not seen as practice until the following summer? Anecdotal evidence can be cited but no account can do justice to the intricacies involved and the complex networks that have to be established for this to happen.

The history of school-centred work that we have given demonstrates, we hope, that teachers' professional development depends on a combination of elements. For us, at Forest Gate, it was important that the Head Teacher, however many reservations she may have felt, created, and maintained, space for teacher-initiated activities which sought to serve both the needs of the students and the teachers. It was important that there was continuity over a long period of time for chairing the central committee, though we acknowledge that other arrangements might have worked also. And it was important that there was a succession of individuals, and small groups of like-minded teachers, who generated the necessary sense of purpose to keep others going.

It may be that, under the GRIST arrangements, teachers will be able to create some of the necessary conditions for school-based INSET to flourish. We discussed in Chapter 15 the way in which Forest Gate Community School is proposing to operate its GRIST scheme and noted that the Staff Development Committee has a specific brief and explicit mechanisms for accountability to the whole staff. Under its arrangements, it should be possible for a variety of initiatives to be planned, and provision made for resourcing them, in ways of which the Language and Learning Committee would have been deeply envious. For example, if planned arrangements for cover had been available, others would have been able to do what Nicki Regan was, with some difficulty, able to arrange for herself.

It is thus heavily ironic that, at a time when schools are being encouraged to set their own INSET agendas and have a degree of control over the ways in which these can be resourced, there are national trends which pull against such teacher autonomy. One is built into the GRIST arrangements themselves which could have the effect of limiting, rather than increasing INSET provision.

Central government priorities, like the control over the purse strings, also seem likely to dominate content. Even those priorities identified by schools and LEAs may be directed towards immediate needs and neglect long-term perspectives. This makes us less than optimistic for the kinds of activities undertaken by the Language and Learning Committee which were of the second kind. We anticipate that people in staff rooms, like the Government, may want immediate results.

The other trend which is destined to have far-reaching effects on the professional development of teachers is the imposition of a national curriculum; determined by a few for the many. On the one hand there will be detailed specification of the foundation subjects and on the other, if experience in other countries is anything to go by, there will be a massive expansion of the textbook industry. Both aspects seem to propose a diminution in the role of the teacher. Even if this is not the intention (we suspect it is) we think that the probable narrowing of the curriculum and a preoccupation with testing at 7, 11, 14, and 16 will have the effect of setting a low ceiling of expectation; exactly the opposite of the declared intention to raise teachers' expectations of what students can achieve.

We find it easy to imagine people concentrating on getting good test results with a consequent loss of involvement in shaping what students learn and why. If this were to be the case there would come to be only one measure of your effectiveness as a teacher: whether, or not, your students reach the attainment targets. This would be a long way from the professional involvements developed in the Committee. It will be very difficult to build up professionalism in teachers who find they are constantly marginalized in the educational enterprise.

We also note that one effect of the GRIST initiative has been to decrease the number of people being seconded to full-time, award-bearing courses for diplomas and the MA degree. A partially hidden element in the work of the Committee was the influence of the attendance of individuals at full and part-time award-bearing courses. We have shown earlier that this was not always beneficial as, for example, when it led to a narrow academic framework for end-of-the-school-day activities. However, we think we should record that, over the years, the reciprocal relationship between academic courses and the work undertaken by the Committee was very productive. Some of the contributions to this book rely on wider reading and argument than was available in the Committee meetings. They have been written with a more rigorous attention to detail than was possible using only the resources available in the school. It would be easy to under-estimate the value to a school, LEA, or for that matter nation, of supporting people who wish to extend their qualifications. Our experience suggests that to view this as being of benefit only to the individuals concerned would be far from the truth. The work of the Committee and its sub-groups would have been significantly diminished if some members had not been studying in addition to their school-based investigations. Conversely, we believe that they were able to contribute to the development of theory in their reports and dissertations. Genuine understanding of concepts and theories requires a close awareness of educational practice.

It is also useful to reflect on the role played by links with professional subject and similar associations in the life of the Committee. A number of teachers fed in ideas from national subject perspectives and, as will already be clear, LATE provided both a forum for testing out ideas and a support system for members of the Committee (not only English teachers). Membership of associations such as the National Anti-Racist Movement in Education (NAME) enabled people to make informed contributions to discussion and ensure we avoided parochialism. Networks of these kinds, like involvement in regional and LEA INSET, have a progressive effect on the confidence of teachers. Contact with other teachers at conferences and on courses enables teachers to encounter new ideas and more fully recognize the value of what they already know.

Research

As the reader will have gathered, we fear that teachers may, in future, be expected to engage in professional development which serves no broader ends than the servicing of a centrally determined curriculum. We do not accept this as a satisfactory scenario and propose that teachers must retain all possible means by which they can maintain their full role. They must remain responsible for the negotiation of the curriculum; building on the knowledge and language ability their students already possess and encouraging them to think and act for themselves. If students are actively to participate in society, they will need more than a prepackaged curriculum handed out by teacher technicians.

For these reasons, among others, we find ourselves insisting on the continuing involvement of teachers in classroom research. The work of the Committee took place against a background of school-focused research projects, and the Schools' Council Language for Learning Project in particular. We felt it gave an important dimension to our work, that it was in parallel with similar activities in other parts of the country and we benefited from contact with outsiders who could reflect back to us some indication of how our activities compared with those being undertaken elsewhere. But most vitally, however inadequately, we were ourselves engaged in research for our own purposes in our own context.

Only by having a teaching profession which is trusted to think for itself and is considered capable of contributing to the development of the curriculum will the quality of education be improved. There is no evidence that a curriculum imposed from on high can meet the needs of today's students and society. There is plenty of evidence that for students to take on new ideas they need teachers who understand what they bring to the classroom in terms of knowledge, skills, and attitudes and build on these. There is a great deal of knowledge about how to select and mediate knowledge which rests with the classroom teacher. It is not merely that they know how to teach; they understand the importance of a negotiated content. Attempts to produce teacher-proof curricula and assessment systems ignore the importance of the texture of classroom relationships and are likely to be successful only in narrowing students' and teachers' horizons.

We are aware that there has been a drastic decline in educational research in general and that only quite small sums are being spent on curriculum development of the kinds which fall within the terms of reference of this book. It is often a matter of getting a number of LEAs into a loose confederation before a 'national' project can begin, and LEAs do not have money for more than small-scale initiatives. So it is no use looking back nostalgically to palmier days when there were many local and national projects in which teachers could participate. In the absence of such central support, teachers have no choice but to do what they can, enlisting LEA support where possible but essentially relying on themselves. In the longer term we think there is a need for research which spans all levels – school, local, regional, and national – but in the shorter term, teachers will have to look to each other for mutual support in activities which, by maintaining teachers' intellectual stake in the curriculum and students' learning, will continue to challenge, and irritate, those who would prefer both students and teachers alike not to ask awkward questions or cite contrary evidence.

Appendix

**SUGGESTIONS FOR THE ROLE OF THE
LANGUAGE AND LEARNING COMMITTEE**

Tentative suggestions for the role of the Committee:

1. A vehicle for interdepartment discussion.
2. Provide the school with a solid foundation of learning theory.
3. To look at the learner and the process of learning.
4. Provide a base for some in-service training.
5. Suggest alternative for lower-school curriculum.
6. Provide written statements for discussion.
7. Engage in active research.

How do we start?
Spend time investigating what the school's present language and
learning policy is:

1. Talks about attitudes and policies of different departments.
2. Seminars on different books and theories and how they relate to
   us.
3. Follow one student around for a day/week?
4. Follow one class around for a day/week?
5. Taping students talking in our groups?
6. Taping our own lessons?
7. Look at books used in different departments and readability
   formulae?
8. Use of work sheets?
9. Writing requirements in different departments?
10. Attitude to dialect etc?
11. Look at different forms of assessment and attitudes to marking?
12. Etc; etc; etc.

John Hickman
16 July 1981

DOCUMENT 2

PROPOSED INTRODUCTION FOR A STAFF BOOKLET ON TALK AND LEARNING

If we define oracy as:

1.   Talking to learn
2.   "   "   think
3.   "   "   make relationships with others
4.   "   "   communicate ideas and feelings

then it becomes obvious that talk of all kinds in our classrooms must be regarded as an integral part of the learning process both on a social and on a cognitive level. Of course, the trouble with talk is that, unlike writing, it can't be collected in, reworked, formally assessed and then take its place in a very concrete programme. So how can we explore the talk that goes on in our classrooms in a constructive way and – in so doing – give it a more realistic and valued place in all aspects of the child's development?

Perhaps first we have to capture the talk as it stands by tape recordings and transcripts so that we can work on our own hard evidence because – although there are already endless published and unpublished examples of kids talking – in order for the research to have real value we had to look at our own students in our own classrooms engaged in activities whose contexts we know.

Once this is established the advantage of having one's own tapes are obvious:

1.   They provide an opportunity to study and reflect upon discourse that would otherwise be a fleeting, ungraspable phenomenon.
2.   Working with other people on one's own transcript brings new dimensions to our own understandings.
3.   The opportunity to reflect enables us to look more positively at talk that we might otherwise dismiss as mere chat. It helps us to isolate and acknowledge the many skills that are used all the time and are often ignored.
4.   Provides a useful starting point for effective planning.
5.   We can explore the strategies that are used to take on new knowledge and new ideas and the ways in which they make use of their own language as a tool for learning.
6.   There is space for teacher intuition.
7.   Social strategies and development can be more easily taken into account.
8.   Medium or long-term taping can give a useful perspective on developing awareness.

9. When teacher talk is involved a tape recording gives us an opportunity to be objective about our own classroom role.

Tentative questions

How does the size and composition of the groups affect the response to the task?

What is the effect of teacher intervention/participation in small-group discussion?

What is the effect of teacher-led class discussion? (How do we analyse teacher talk?)

What is the effect that different tasks have on the levels of discourse?
- When does a reworking of the task occur?
- When is anecdote seen to be at its most effective?
- How is the initiative placed in the hands of the student?

How do we arrive at an appreciation of the social and cognitive strategies used and the development in each of these areas?

Can the same task with different age ranges provide us with an insight into development of various skills?

DOCUMENT 3

SUGGESTED ACTIVITIES BASED ON *IMPROVING SECONDARY SCHOOLS*
Language and learning committee

At our last meeting John McGill introduced the Hargreaves' Report and it has been agreed that we should each take a small section and present it to the Committee during the next two terms.

The main part of the report divides up easily into sixteen sections which I have listed below. It would be very useful if each member of the committee (and anyone else who is interested) could note down their first, second and third choices for presentation and I can then allocate sections accordingly.

I'd be very grateful if you could put this form into my pigeon hole a.s.a.p.

John Hickman

Please put down your 1st 3 choices in order of preference.

The Teacher-Parent Partnership School Attendance The Transition from Primary to Secondary The Whole Curriculum Pupil Grouping Pupils with particular needs and aptitudes ESL & Bilingual (or multi-lingual) Pupils Skills for Independent Learning The 4th & 5th Year: Core & Options The 4th & 5th Year: Active Learning Roles The 4th & 5th Year: Organizing & Assessing the Curriculum Pupil involvement & participation Learning out of School School & Community Schools, Industry & the Trades Unions Alternative Provision	

Signed: _____

N.B. Our next meeting is on Monday, 21 January.

DOCUMENT 4

LANGUAGE SURVEY FORM

Our Languages

1. What is your name? _____
2. What form are you in? _____
3. Can you *understand* any language other than English ☐ Yes
   ☐ No
4. If you answered 'yes' to the last question, fill in the chart below:

Write down the languages you *understand* apart from English	Tick the box below if you can also *speak* this language	Tick the box below if you *read* this language	Tick the box below if you can *write* this language
(1)			
(2)			
(3)			
(4)			

161

5. Who do you speak to in a language other than English? (e.g. friends, mother, neighbour) _____
6. Are you studying any languages apart from English in school?

    ☐ Yes
    ☐ No

7. If you answered 'yes' to the last question, what languages are you studying? _____
8. What other languages apart from English, do people in your class speak? _____

DOCUMENT 5

FINAL LETTER TO MEMBERS OF THE LANGUAGE AND LEARNING COMMITTEE

Dear

I am sending this letter to anyone who has either participated in or shown any form of interest in the Language and Learning Committee over the past seven years.

The committee has had a varied and sometimes transient membership and has engaged in a large number of activities which I feel have been of benefit to the school in fairly subtle ways.

Unfortunately I think the time has come to think in terms of other organizational structures for the sorts of things that went on in the Language & Learning Committee.

There are a number of reasons for this:

1. Withdrawal of goodwill over the past four years has meant that momentum has frequently been lost and the ensuing staccato activity is fatal to a committee of this nature.
2. The wisdom of Mr Baker will ensure continued disruption and it would be very difficult to rely on the Committee's activities being a part of our 'directed' time.
3. Increasing commitments elsewhere have meant that the Committee has dropped even lower in the list of everyone's priorities – including mine!
4. Related to the last point is the fact that activities have, increasingly, been orchestrated from the chair and this is a distortion of the original intention of the Committee.
5. My new GRIST role is one that is going to take up most of my 'spare' time if it is to be, in any way, a positive influence in school.
6. GRIST does offer immense opportunities for people to take

control of their own In-Service needs and professional development and many of the activities engaged in by members of the committee in the past can now be taken on with the aid of GRIST funding and built into the school's yearly Institutional Development Plans (IDPs).

I intend to form a staff development committee which will be a forum for INSET ideas, initiatives and planning and I hope that members of the Language and Learning Committee will involve themselves in this new venture which I will outline in a separate letter.

On a positive note, Routledge & Kegan Paul Ltd have agreed to publish a book on the history and work of the committee and this seems a very good way to wind up such a productive period of seven years.

Thanks to everyone who has contributed in any way to the numerous successes of the Committee. I look forward to your involvement in GRIST.

John Hickman
June 1987

DOCUMENT 6

REPORT ON INSET SESSION ON COMMUNITY PERSPECTIVES

There were five members of the panel:

Mrs Ashraf	Parent governor at Forest Gate
N.N. Begum	Newham resident
Mr Dhesi	Newham teacher of community languages
Pandit Narayan	Haringey teacher/Newham resident
Ms Yap Hi Chu	Camden Chinese Community Centre

Each contributor gave a five-minute perspective on the background of children from their particular language/religious community, giving some pointers towards areas of potential confusion or difficulty which might arise for pupils in school. What follows is a brief summary of points raised.

Appendix

Sikh Community

Mr Dhesi spoke from the perspective of the Panjabi-speaking and Sikh community:

Many children come from families who had a rural background in India and who were raised under a colonial education system. They tend to accord teachers prestige and have expectations of a formal educational style. Generally not accustomed to the emphasis on socialisation which the British system now gives, they perhaps require particular explanation/reassurance in this area.

Most children will have experience of Panjabi, and the range of communicative styles used in the language, even if they cannot read or write it. Formal expectations.

The Panjabi/Sikh community in Britain is increasingly adopting Western-style family units.

The naming patterns of Sikhism are important. A name is given to a child several weeks after birth, and the naming will be part of a religious ceremony. It is not arbitrarily chosen by the parents, but derived from an initial letter given by the Sikh holy book (Guru Granth Sahib).

Muslim Community

Mrs Ashraf spoke from the point of view of the Muslim, Urdu-speaking community:

There are changing patterns of expectations which are emerging as the patterns of social integration change: the original purpose of many immigrants from Pakistan was to earn money. As families have decided to settle, their perspectives have shifted towards greater involvement in British society. Where women would not once have felt a need to learn English, for instance, they are now increasingly doing so.

Similarly, naming is moving away from the traditional religious patterns towards adoption of family surnames in European style.

Families are less on the extended pattern than formerly.

Islam is viewed as a code for living: it permeates every aspect of life.

There will generally be fairly formal expectations of teachers: Muslim families would expect children to respect teachers and teachers to discipline their pupils. There should be close liaison between parents and teachers.

164

Bangladeshi Community

N.N. Begum spoke from the point of view of the Bangladeshi Muslim community:

The majority of Bangladeshi parents are not literate and do not have expectations of the education system based on previous experience. This is an area which requires consideration by the school, as parents find approaching the school a difficult matter.

There is a high rate of unemployment amongst the Bangladeshi community.

There is urgent need for the Bangladeshi community to be supported in the development of literacy in the first language (Bangla) in order to bridge the educational gap which currently exists.

Many children, and their parents, experience difficulty in understanding the differences in words which were originally absorbed into Bangla but which have evolved with pronunciation/emphasis different from the English variety. It is a huge source of confusion.

Naming patterns still follow traditional customs so that individuals do not necessarily share names with parents or children, or brothers with sisters. It is crucial for the school to discover both the correct names of children and others in their family.

Hindu Community

Pandit Narayan spoke from the perspective of the Hindu community:

There is need to relieve the burden on parents to maintain the Mother Tongue in a formal way for their children; many parents do not have the educational background or expertise to undertake this responsibility.

Responsibility rests with the school for three main reasons:

- it contributes to the development of respect for different cultures in school
- it contributes to the development of pupils' self-identity
- it enhances the educational potential of bilingual pupils and would ultimately have a positive impact on achievement at GCSE/A levels

The cultural background of Hinduism emphasises non-violence and as part of this, a vegetarian diet.

Chinese Community

Ms Yap Hi Chu spoke from the perspective of the Chinese-speaking community:

Many points raised by the other speakers equally apply to Chinese speakers.

Many people who have come to Britain from China have not come from the city of Hong Kong but from Kowloon which is on the border. Theirs is a rural background and many people are not literate.

There is potential confusion with Chinese in that although a name might be spelt in Chinese characters similarly across the country, its pronunciation varies according to region. Thus transliterated names in English look as if they are different whereas they might in fact be the same.

Chinese names place the family name at the beginning: Yap is Ms Yap Hi Chu's family name. Some families have adopted the European convention but others retain the Chinese form. This needs to be checked with new pupils.

Difficulties in the acquisition of English language arise from key features of Chinese:

- the sound system is monosyllabic; words do not elide sounds as they do in English
- there is no gender distinction
- there are no past and present tenses as such: past time is denoted by other means
- there is a predominance of guttural sound

As with Bangla, there has been an evolution of absorbed vocabulary from English.

The cultural background of many families in the Chinese community is in the catering trade; this has implications for the involvement of parents in the school. Time precludes parental attendance at meetings. Parents do not demand a great deal of the school; they very much leave the job of education to the teachers. The idea that they should be involved is new and will take time to be assimilated.

As long as there is no maintenance of the mother tongue, English will persist in being a difficulty.

There is a need for continued pressure to make mother tongue provision in school for the Chinese community. This would underpin cultural identity of the community.

DOCUMENT 7

SCHOOL POLICY STATEMENT

Every member of Forest Gate is held to be of equal value. We should demonstrate this fact in all facets of school life but most particularly in respect of racial prejudice and racial abuse. This is an area in which there must be no ambiguity concerning the school's attitude and the response of the staff.

It is therefore vital that this ethos be reflected in the curriculum and conduct of the school and that we should at all times be sensitive to the issues involved and seek to improve our strategies as teachers for eliminating prejudice and encouraging respect for all individuals, races and nationalities.

Incidents of racialist behaviour must be reported immediately to the Head of Year and will be deemed to constitute unacceptable or even dangerous behaviour. The appropriate sanction will be imposed accordingly. It is recognized that this is not simply a disciplinary matter but will require subsequent follow-up and counselling.

Racialist views and behaviour are particularly destructive of the fabric of our community. The problem should not therefore be categorized simply as a matter requiring disciplinary sanctions.

Staff at Forest Gate are expected to work with pupils and parents in expressing a positive and committed approach to promoting issues of multi-culturalism in general and in showing no equivocation in dealing with racism whenever and however it occurs.

Our growth and development as a community and as individuals are dependent on our mutual respect and support: as staff our example, particularly in consistency of attitude and conduct, is paramount in the education of our students.

A. Rowland
Headteacher

An Equal Opportunity Employer

NEWHAM'S ANTI-RACIST SHORT STATEMENT

The London Borough of Newham is committed to achieving equality
in its education service. This means an education service made free
from racism and prejudice so that the Authority can meet the needs
of everyone in our community.

Many reports have shown how racism affects education. What is
racism? Racism is a mixture of prejudice and discrimination, plus the
power to affect others with it. Since power is mainly in the hands of
white people, it means that black people and ethnic minorities are the
victims of prejudice. For example, the idea, that black people are not
as good as white people, is a common attitude. We all need to
understand how these racist ideas come about and work towards
getting rid of racism for the good of everyone.

How does racism work? First of all there are very few black people
in a position to make decisions within the system. Black people's
views must be taken into account when making policy. Secondly,
some discrimination is deliberate and includes personal abuse, graffiti
and racist attacks by members of one group on another. Thirdly,
some procedures and attitudes within the education service reduce
opportunities for ethnic minorities. These need to be identified and
changed.

The Race Relations Act of 1976 places a duty on every local
authority to stop racial discrimination and to promote good relations
between black and white people. Therefore, the Local Education
Authority in Newham is asking all Schools and Colleges to make and
publicise statements against racism. Also the Governing Bodies
should review action taken in schools to meet the needs of a multi-
ethnic society. Lastly, the Education Service itself should ensure that
any administrative procedures do not discriminate against members
of ethnic minority groups.

The Authority is committed to promoting equality of opportunity
and good race relations.

Andrew Lockhart, M.A.
Acting Director of Education
23 October 1985

DOCUMENT 9

Non-Sexist Education: Policy Statement

The London Borough of Newham believes in the inherent equality of all individuals irrespective of their sex. It recognises, however, that individuals are not always treated as equals and that women and girls experience discrimination and disadvantage because of their sex. Some groups, for example, black women and girls, and women with disabilities, face double discrimination. This situation is maintained by political, social and economic systems, and is reinforced by, amongst other things, the education system.

The Council intends its education system to be one which challenges this current unjust state of affairs. It commits itself to:

- a review of all educational philosophy and practice within the Borough to ensure true equality of opportunity for both sexes
- the elimination of all practices which discriminate unfairly between the sexes
- a review of recruitment and promotion procedures to ensure equal opportunities for staff
- the involving of all parties concerned with education within the Borough in the implementing of its equal opportunities policy statement
- the support of individuals and institutions implementing this policy statement
- the development of procedures for the effective dealing with incidents of sexual harassment
- the evaluation of all of the above to ensure that continuous progress is made towards non-sexist education for all students

The Council believes that good education is by definition non-sexist and that the elimination of sexism will benefit both sexes. It regards the achievement of a non sexist education service, therefore, as a matter of the utmost urgency.

Distributed by INSEC

LONDON BOROUGH OF NEWHAM
EDUCATION DEPARTMENT   An Equal Opportunity Authority

Bibliography

Adelman, C. (ed.) *Uttering, Muttering: Collecting, Using and Reporting Talk for Social and Education Research*, London, Grant McIntyre, 1981

Barnes, D. *From Communication to Curriculum*, Harmondsworth, Penguin, 1976

Barnes, D. and Todd, F. *Communication and Learning in Small Groups*, London, Routledge and Kegan Paul, 1977

Barnes, D. et al. *Language, the Learner and the School*, Harmondsworth, Penguin, 1969, revised edition 1986

Berlak, A. and Berlak, H. *Dilemmas of Schooling: Teaching and Social Change*, London, Methuen, 1981

Brice Heath, S. *Ways with Words: Language, Life, and Work in Communities and Classrooms*, Cambridge, Cambridge University Press, 1983

Britton, J. *Language and Learning*, London, Allen Lane, 1970

Cashdan, A. and Grugeon, E. (eds) *Language in Education*, London, Routledge and Kegan Paul, 1972

Chorny, M. (ed.) *Teacher as Learner*, University of Calgary Department of Curriculum and Instruction, Alberta, 1985

Department of Education and Science, *A Language for Life*, London, HMSO, 1975

West Indian Children in Our Schools: Interim Report of the Committee of Enquiry into the Education of Children from Ethnic Minority Groups, London, HMSO, 1981

Bullock Revisited: a discussion paper by HMI, London, HMSO, 1982

Curriculum Matters: English from 5 to 16, HMSO, 1984

Duffy, M. 'The End of a Partnership', *Times Educational Supplement*, 18 September 1987, p. 29

Edwards, A.D. *Language in Culture and Class: The Sociology of Language and Education*, London, Heinemann Educational, 1976

Edwards, A.D. and Furlong, V.J. *The Language of Teaching*, London, Heinemann, 1978

Edwards, D. & Mercer, N. *Common Knowledge: The Development of Understanding in the Classroom*, London, Methuen, 1987

Edwards, V. *Language in Multicultural Classrooms*, London, Batsford, 1983

Evans, G. 'The School as a Centre of Professional Development', in Skilbeck, M. (ed.) *Readings in School-based Curriculum Development*, London, Harper Education, 1984

Gillham, B. (ed.) *The Language of School Subjects*, London, Heinemann, 1986

Greene, M. *Teacher as Stranger*, Wadsworth Publishing Company, 1973

Gundara, J., Jones, C. and Kimberley, K. (eds) *Racism, Diversity and Education*, London, Hodder and Stoughton, 1986

Hargreaves, D.H. *The Challenge for the Comprehensive School: Culture, Curriculum and Community*, London, Routledge and Kegan Paul, 1982 *Classroom Studies, Educational Analysis*, Vol. 2, No. 2, Winter, 1980

Hebdige, D. 'Reggae Rastas and Rudies' in Hall, S. and Jefferson, T. (eds) *Resistance through Rituals: youth subcultures in post-war Britain*, London, Hutchinson in association with Centre for Contemporary Cultural Studies, University of Birmingham, 1976

Hickman, G.M., Reynolds, J.B. and Tolley, H. *A New Professionalism for a Changing Geography*, Schools' Council, 1974

Inner London Education Authority *Improving Secondary Schools* (The Hargreaves' Report), ILEA, 1984

Lee, J. *School-based Staff Development Activities: A Handbook for Secondary Schools*, York, Longman for Schools' Council, 1984

Levine, N. *Language Teaching and Learning: History*, London, Ward Lock, 1981

Linguistic Minorities Project, *The Other Languages of England*, London, Routledge and Kegan Paul, 1985

McLeod, A. and Richmond, J. 'Craft and Art', *The English Magazine*, 6, Spring 1981, The English Centre, Inner London Education Authority, 1981

Martin, N., Williams, P., Wilding, J., Hemmings, S., Medway, P. *Understanding Children Talking*, Harmondsworth, Penguin, 1976

Medway, P. 'The Bible and the Vernacular: The Significance of Language Across the Curriculum', *English in Education*, Vol. 15, No. 1, pp. 3-7, 1981

Meek, M. et. al. *Achieving Literacy*, London, Routledge and Kegan Paul, 1983

Miller, J. *Many Voices*, London, Routledge and Kegan Paul, 1983

Nixon, J. (ed.) *A Teacher's Guide to Action Research*, London, Open Books, 1979

Nixon, J., Magee, F. and Sheard, D. *Teachers in Research*, London, Schools Council Publication, 1979.

Nuttall, D. (1981), *School Self-evaluation: Accountability with a human face*, York, Longmans, 1981

Oldroyd, D., Smith, K. and Lee, J. *School-based Staff Development Activities: A Handbook for Secondary Schools*, York, Longman, 1984

Rassool, N. *Bilingualism . . . a radical critique*, MA Dissertation, King's College, London, 1986.

Richmond, J. *The Resources of Classroom Language*, London, Edward Arnold, 1982

Robertson, I. *Language Across the Curriculum: Four Case Studies*, Schools Council Working Paper No. 67, London, Methuen, 1980

Rosen, H. 'The Language of Text-Books', in Britton, J. (ed.) *Talking and Writing*, London, Methuen, 1967

Rosen, H. and Burgess, T. *Languages and Dialects of London School*

   Children: an Investigation, London, Ward Lock, 1980
Rosen, H. and Rosen, C. *The Language of Primary School Children*, Harmondsworth, Penguin, 1973
Rudduck, J. 'Curriculum Development and Teacher Research', in Silbeck, M. (ed.), *Readings in School-based Curriculum Development*, London, Harper Education, 1984
   (ed.) *Teachers in Partnership: four studies of in-service collaboration*, York, Longman, 1982
SCDC publications, National Oracy Project Planning Brief, September 1987.
Stenhouse, L. *An Introduction to Curriculum Research and Development*, London, Heinemann, 1975
Stubbs, M. and Delamont, S. *Explorations in Classroom Observation*, New York, Wiley, 1976
Stubbs, M. *Educational Linguistics*, London, Blackwell, 1986
Talk Workshop Group, *Becoming Our Own Experts*, London, 1982
Thomson, L. and A. *What Learning Looks Like*, York, Longman, 1984
Tolley, H. and Reynolds, J.B. *Geography 14-18: a handbook for school-based curriculum development*, Schools' Council/Macmillan Education, 1977
Torbe, M. *Language Policies in Action*, London, Ward Lock, 1980
Torbe, M. and Medway P. *Language Teaching and Learning: The Climate for Learning*, London, Ward Lock, 1981.
Yarde, R. 'New currents in Docklands', *Times Higher Educational Supplement*, 3.7.87

Index

FGS abbreviation refers to Forest Gate School

173